FROM
Beaver Creek To Hanoi

A Mother's Quest to Rescue Her Son

CHERYL GRANT GILLESPIE

In Collaboration with Markham & Marcia Gartley

*"I do not underestimate the power of prayer - but the Walls of Jericho
did not fall until the Israelites had marched around them
seven times, and blown their trumpets. We must do the same!!!"*

Minnie Lee Gartley to the League of Families of POWs/MIAs, 1971

FROM BEAVER CREEK TO HANOI:
A Mother's Quest to Rescue Her Son

Author's Note: This is a work of nonfiction written in narrative form.

For further information and permission approval or to order copies of this book, go to https://cheryl-writes.com.

Androscoggin Press, West Kennebunk, Maine

ISBN #979-8-9866181-0-4

Printed in the United States of America

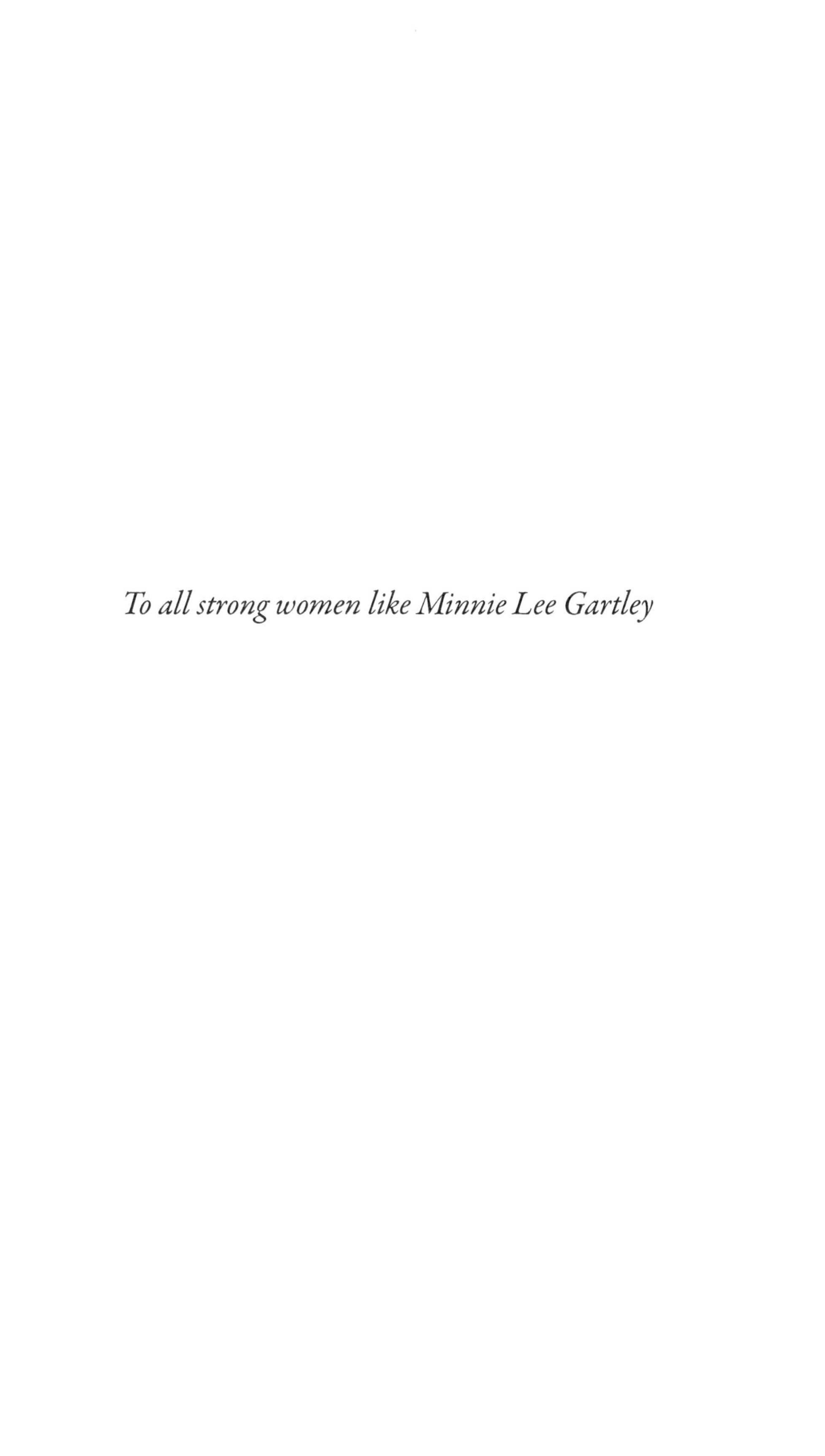

To all strong women like Minnie Lee Gartley

PROLOGUE

THIS IS THE STORY OF THREE YEARS and one month of
Minnie Lee Ligon Gartley's life, taking place between August of 1969 and
September of 1972. It was part of a larger, unsettling, and divisive period of
time for the United States. If you were born after 1970, you might agree with
people who say there has never been a more discordant time in our country as
the period between the 2010s to the present. Those of us who are old enough
to remember the 1960s spilling into the 1970s often smile at that notion,
remembering that tumultuous period of political revolt, social changes, and
economic upheaval.

Assassinations of politicians and civil rights workers filled the news. We
saw the assassinations of President John Kennedy and his brother presidential
candidate and Senator Robert Kennedy. Civil rights leader Martin Luther
King, Jr. and lesser-known civil rights figures lost their lives. We ate supper to
nightly news stories filled with recounts of battles and death tolls of the war
in Vietnam and the rest of Indochina.

President Lyndon Johnson, who succeeded President Kennedy, brought
many social programs into existence, such as his War on Poverty and the
signing of the Civil Rights Act. Regrettably, he was unable to deal with the
military intervention in Vietnam to the satisfaction of the people in America.
Torn between war hawks who felt the war could be brought to an honorable
end by simply bombing the hell out of Vietnam and peaceniks who just
wanted to pull everyone out and bring them home, Johnson could not find
a happy medium. The former group hollered "my country, right or wrong,"
while the latter chanted "make love, not war." Johnson's next term was filled
with protests, student demonstrations, and sit-ins against the war. By the
end of his presidency, he was beseeched by wives and families of POWs and
MIAs of the war being held in North Vietnam while trying desperately to

negotiate a peace with the North Vietnamese. President Johnson decided not to run for president again.

The year of 1968 was plagued with horrific upheaval in the United States. A six day riot in the Watts section of Los Angeles, that sprang from a twenty-one year old black man suffering police abuse, left thirty-four people dead, over one thousand injured, and forty million dollars' worth of property damage. Protests and riots concerning frustrations with social injustices and the continuation of the war in Vietnam happened across the country.

Also that summer of 1968, Ltjg. Markham Ligon Gartley and his navigator Lt. William Mayhew were shot down over North Vietnam on August 17th during Operation Rolling Thunder, the bombing of North Vietnam started by President Johnson in 1965. Mark and Bill's parents would not find out what happened to them for a long time.

Presidential candidate Hubert Humphry was beaten by Richard Nixon who campaigned on bringing peace with honor to Vietnam and stopping the violence within our own borders. President Nixon continued Operation Rolling Thunder after taking office and also implemented a lottery for drafting young men into the military. Protests continued here in the United States. One at Kent State University in the spring of 1970 left four students dead as National Guardsmen fired on the demonstrators.

The average American, who was not involved in the war directly, or part of the segment of people protesting it, grew tired of the Vietnam situation and seemed to want to forget it. Unfortunately, the war was not over for people with family members in Southeast Asia still fighting, being held as prisoners, or missing in action.

As this book begins, Minnie Lee finds out news about her missing son Mark and decides to become involved in working with organizations trying to do something about the war situation. She eventually finds herself dealing with opposing political ends of the Vietnam issue, both groups supportive of the administration's war efforts and peace groups working against them to save her Mark and others. Her grace, intelligence, and eloquence of speech served her well as she worked relentlessly for their release from prisoner of war camps. This is the story of her courageous journey from her home in Beaver Creek, Maine to Hanoi, North Vietnam.

CHAPTER 1

The Letter

Minnie Lee Gartley stood stock-still at the kitchen sink of the cabin at Beaver Creek Camps in Maine. It was a hot August day, 1969. Her hands, held to her face, smelled of Ajax from cleaning. That scent mixed with the room's other odors—a potpourri of burnt fire wood, drying waders, fishing baskets, and pine— was the familiar smell of summer work at the camps her husband Gerry and she ran on Moosehead Lake. Minnie Lee, or Min Lee as family and close friends often called her, was finding it hard to get work done that day. She had spent the last year trying to get herself to accept the fact that Gerry's and her much wanted, first-born son Markham was missing-in-action in Vietnam and possibly dead. He'd been shot down just like her first husband whom Min Lee had lost during World War II; a husband she had kept a secret from everyone except Gerry and her childhood family in Kentucky. No one here in Maine knew this could be a double loss for Min Lee, including her two sons.

Markham, or Mark as most people called him, was a handsome child born in May of 1944 and named after Min Lee's father Markham Ligon.

Blonde, hazel-eyed, and always with a smile on his face, he charmed people at the campground as a boy running around doing errands for his parents. An athlete in school, Mark graduated as the valedictorian of his high school class. After graduating from Georgia Tech where he had received a full ROTC Navy scholarship and was battalion commander his senior year, Mark informed his parents he was going into Naval Aviation to be a pilot, a top gun. Min Lee told him she wished he wouldn't do that, but Mark thought she was probably just being protective and proceeded with his plans. He wrote to his parents about the thrill of flying an F-4 phantom jet off the USS Constellation. After he finished his training, he hadn't been flying bombing raids in Operation Rolling Thunder for long when Min Lee and Gerry stopped hearing from him. After no word from him since August of 1968, they received a letter from the military in January of 1969 explaining that someone observed Mark and his navigator Bill Mayhew eject successfully from their plane after it was hit. The letter also said nothing more was known about what happened to them. The endless period of not knowing any specific details that followed had been excruciating. Min Lee had tried to ignore the calendar in the camp kitchen that reminded her it was August again, but this morning she paused and took a good look at it. Mark had been gone for a full year now. The tough shell Min Lee had tried to keep around her heart cracked slightly. And it ached.

"Min!"

"For God's sake, Gerry! You scared me half to death!" answered Min Lee, without turning around to look at her husband. "What are you doing here so early? Thought you'd be out longer with that fishing group." Min Lee fussed with a dish towel at the edge of the sink while trying to wipe her eyes. When she finally pivoted and saw Gerry's face, she noticed her usually stoic husband looked rattled somehow.

"Min, the worker from the camp store brought this up just now. Caught me outside running up to grab some more lures for the guys to use at the dock. He was curious about the Chicago return address on the envelope. It's addressed simply to "Gartley, Greenville, Maine." Gerry paused and placed something down on the long, pine camp table and looked up. "Min, it's him!"

"What are you talking about, Gerry?"

"Look!" Gerry pointed to what looked like a page torn out from a magazine on the table. "It's Mark, Min!"

Min Lee walked over to the table and peeked at the page. It was a picture of men somewhere tropical. She looked closer. One did look like Mark. The caption under the picture had three words in English—Mark Ham Gartley. Min Lee looked closer at the picture. There was also a letter that had fallen out onto the table. Min Lee didn't need to read that right now. It was him. Her handsome son. He was alive? In a prisoner of war camp, but alive?

Min Lee spent a few seconds rubbing the tip of her right index finger on Mark's face in the photo. Then she hugged herself. She couldn't process this. The magazine photo cracked the shell around her heart wide open.

"Oh, Gerry," whispered Min Lee. "Why haven't we heard anything from someone official?" Her pragmatic husband kept telling her to expect the worst about Mark after all this time. Now this?

"Min, I don't know any better than you."

"I need a minute," said Min Lee as Gerry tried to approach her with one arm extended in her direction. She ran out of the camp and down to the shore of Moosehead Lake. With shaky hands, she whacked a cigarette out of the pack she kept in her apron pocket and lit it after four attempts and some curse words. Raised on a peach and tobacco farm in Kentucky, Min Lee took solace in smoking a cigarette, but today it wasn't working as well as it usually did. The massive stretch of open water before her did not have the calming effect it always gave her either. After a few puffs, she threw her half-finished cigarette to the ground and stomped it out. She shook herself and realized she might want to read the letter with the magazine. She hustled back up to the camp and found Gerry still standing at the table and simply looking at the picture. Min Lee grabbed the letter, unfolded it, and read aloud:

Dear Mr. and Mrs. Gartley,

We get a magazine from Poland which is where my husband and I are from. We were interested in this picture of the American POWs. The only name they seemed to have gotten in English was Mark Ham Gartley. In the article it said this Mark's parents were from Greenville, Maine, so we tried sending it this way.

If this is not a relative of yours, please forgive us.

Sincerely,
Mr. and Mrs. Kowalczyk

"Good heavens," said Min Lee under her breath. Then she said a bit louder, "How did this couple get this information when you and I have heard nothing from the military, Gerry? How?"

Gerry shrugged his shoulders. "I have no idea, Min. No damned idea at all. But he's alive. Min, he's alive. At least he was when this picture was taken." They stood quietly for a few minutes until they heard a call from outside.

"Gartley, where are those lures?"

"Min?"

"I know, Gerry. Bring them the lures. We'll talk later. I need to let Jim know. Get going now."

Before Gerry came in with the news of Mark, Min Lee was planning to start getting ready to go back to Dunedin, Florida, to their mobile home where she lived while teaching high school history and civics. Gerry would eventually shut the Maine camp down for the winter and join her in the warmer state. She and Gerry had done this double residency ever since Mark had gone off to college. Their second son Jim, diagnosed a few years earlier with bipolar disorder, went back and forth with his mother as he needed her support. Min Lee helped Jim get into therapy groups, find odd jobs, and take some college classes in Florida. There were so many services down there to help Jim with his problems. Gerry would return to Beaver Creek for the start of fishing season in the spring as soon as the ice was out of Moosehead Lake. Min Lee and Jim would go up to Maine when school closed down in Dunedin. It was an arrangement that worked for them. Min Lee considered those Maine winters brutal when she had taught at Greenville High School, and Gerry struggled with his younger son's illness.

Min Lee soothed herself by thinking about the fact that she would have more time and better resources to study the POW situation once she was settled in Florida. This war, or military action since war was not officially declared, puzzled her. A patriotic soul, she had been a WAC during World War II stationed at Fort Knox with her second husband Gerry and would have stayed longer than a year and a half if her mother hadn't taken ill. She was honorably discharged to go care for her. There was a purpose to the war in the 1940s. Everyone seemed to support it. The United States' intervention in Vietnam was chaotic. The media was filled with contradictions about why the U.S. was there and what they were doing for that country. Even the well-respected news anchor Walter Cronkite had openly criticized the U.S. involvement there over a year ago. Min Lee was startled when he spoke like that during his news broadcast, and she still thought about it now. The news was paying more attention to student protests and huge music festivals like Woodstock this summer than they were paying to the ongoing battle in Southeast Asia. Min Lee knew she had to get involved with the political debate. She had started questioning the purpose of the war before Mark went to Vietnam. She wasn't going to just sit back and wait to see what would happen with Mark now. That's for sure.

CHAPTER 2

Dunedin

Traffic was always heavy on Interstate 95 just before hitting the D.C. area. Min Lee was busy talking about her feelings concerning Vietnam. Her younger son Jim was not interested. He slouched as he rode shotgun in the overstuffed car they were cruising south in.

"I don't know what's going on in the war. First Nixon starts going into Cambodia then he starts talking about troop withdrawal." She glanced sideways. Quelling a feeling of irritation, Min Lee reminded herself that Jim simply didn't have the ability to debate politics. Min Lee knew Jim had problems long before his official diagnosis. His obsessive compulsion about arranging his toys at a young age had worried her. Taunting by his peers once he started school had upset her. Even with the problem named, "help" really wasn't helping much. The so-called treatments were hard on him. *Damned those electro shock treatments,* she thought to herself. *As if her Jim wasn't withdrawn enough before receiving those!*

Jim sighed.

Silence.

Traffic stopped suddenly in front of them. Both Min Lee and Jim were thrown forward as she braked. "Are you okay?" she asked Jim.

"Yes, Mom. When will we be able to stop for lunch?"

Min Lee put her head against the steering wheel. Horns barked behind her. She picked her head up, squared her shoulders, and started driving again while cursing under her breath.

"Mom?"

"It's okay, Jim. We'll stop soon."

Their mobile home in Dunedin was stifling when Min Lee and Jim arrived a day later. They had come from wearing sweatshirts and sitting around a camp fire in the north woods, so this temperature seemed unbearable. Jim ran around opening windows while his mother told him not to and tried desperately to turn the air conditioning up. They decided to go out to grab something to eat while the place cooled down once the AC finally rumbled louder.

With a hamburger and fries spread out in front of him, Jim looked across the booth at his mother. He wiped his mouth with the back of his hand. Min Lee scowled at him, so he picked up a napkin. She studied Jim's face. Mark was six years old when his little brother came along. The age difference made it difficult for the boys to be close. Min Lee had tried to help them develop a better relationship, but Gerry had always said things like "it is what it is."

Min Lee smiled at Jim. "Want another burger?"

Min Lee loved being close to everything they needed when they were staying in their mobile home park in Dunedin. The next morning before the heat of the day, she dressed, attended to her hair and a little makeup, and placed a favorite hat on her head before setting out for a day of research. She walked the three tenths of a mile over to the high school where she taught. School wasn't officially open yet, but she knew the librarian would be there getting everything ready. In the coolness of the research section, Min scoured newspapers for war protests and mention of prominent anti-war activists. The librarian left her alone for a while, but she eventually made her way over to Min Lee's table.

"I was thrilled to hear through the grapevine about Mark," said the librarian upon reaching the library table where Min Lee had several newspapers spread out.

"Thanks, it was a shock to find out that way." Min Lee told her about the Polish magazine.

"I don't believe that! There's so much about this war the average person knows nothing about. What exactly are you looking for today?"

Min Lee glanced around the library and then replied, "I'm checking out war protestors."

The librarian pulled out a chair next to Min Lee and sat down. "I have to be careful what I have in here because of the students, but the public library would have some good material on some of the folks who have been anti-war since the end of World War II. Do you know the names of any good anti-war groups?"

Min Lee leaned in closer. "I want a group that is not just unruly kids. A group that is working toward something instead of just against things. Does that exist?"

"I recently read about one that I think you might find interesting. Women Strike for Peace. Been around since the early 60s. Can't remember any of the leaders names, but I read that Coretta Scott King belongs to it. Can't be too way out there."

"No, they can't," said Min Lee shaking her head. "Think they'd have info on it at the public library, do you?"

"Have your car with you today?"

"Jim has it doing some errands for us. Bit of a walk in the heat. I'll go tomorrow after dropping him off at his group meeting. Thanks!"

Both women stood up at the same time and smoothed their sundresses. The librarian smiled briefly and then spoke seriously, "Min Lee, you need to be careful about talking to people around school about this investigation of war protestors. You never know what others are thinking. There are still people on staff and in administration who are pro-war. Hate to see you have any trouble over it."

"You're right. Feelings and beliefs are still all over the place, and all these demonstrations and riots in the past couple years have divided people even more. Discretion is the word." Min Lee said goodbye, left the library, and fretted all the way back home about handling this whole mess. This country was a divisive disaster about the Vietnam situation. As her Mark sat imprisoned in North Vietnam, other young men were volunteering to go there to serve while others were talking about going to Canada to avoid the draft that was being considered. A draft considered by a president who claimed he would end the war while he was campaigning. The absurdity of all this made Min Lee's head spin, and she was glad to get back to her mobile home and into the coolness of the air conditioning.

CHAPTER 3

Women Strike for Peace

The next morning brought a blast of heat and humidity to Dunedin. Min Lee was glad she had planned to drop Jim off at his group counseling session and keep the car to drive to the public library. Her clothes were clinging to her skin from sweat she worked up just getting to the car from the trailer and waiting for the air conditioning to kick in as they drove along. Jim jumped out quickly at his stop. Min Lee was in the parking lot of the library by the time the car was cool, so she placed her hat firmly on her head to block the sun as much as possible and braced herself before opening the side door for a run to the building. The quiet coolness of the huge building soothed her. She usually did her own research, but today she felt a sense of urgency.

"Do you know where I might find information about the group Women Strike for Peace, please?" Min Lee asked as she leaned against the marble front desk.

The young woman behind the counter looked up from her desk. "Could you repeat that, Ma'am?"

Min Lee sighed. "Women Strike for Peace."

"I have no idea, I'm afraid. Perhaps periodicals? The microfiche room is…"

"I know, I know," Min Lee interrupted. She shook her head and hustled off to it and asked another librarian for recent Washington Post issues. She was pleasantly surprised to find an article in the Post about a meeting for Women Strike for Peace back in September 29, 1961. Other meetings were mentioned as well, including a demonstration in front of the White House on January 15, 1962. That day nearly 2,000 women gathered in the rain. After that demonstration, President Kennedy said in a news conference that he "saw the ladies through the window and their message was received."[1] Min Lee paused at that point and wondered why she had never heard of this organization before now. Why didn't these women get more press?

Min Lee learned that this group had been formed by Bella Abzug and Dagmar Wilson in 1961 to oppose the development of nuclear weapons at the peak of the Cold War.[2] They had held conferences and protests and were falsely accused of supporting communism. In 1964 at their fourth national conference in San Francisco, they adopted a resolution opposing the military action taking place in Vietnam.

One name in particular seemed to come up often in the articles about this peace group—Ethel Barol Taylor, or Mrs. William Taylor as she identified herself to the police when she wanted to sound "respectable." In one article, she was referred to as the "rebel in white gloves." Min Lee liked that and thought she looked about her age in the pictures. She was an affluent sculptor who had organized the Philadelphia chapter of this peace group. Skimming through the article, Min Lee learned that Women Strike for Peace, or WSP for short, was interested in promoting peace and protesting the development of nuclear weapons and not involved in the feminist issues or the civil rights movement of the time. Min Lee liked that. She was a woman who spoke her mind and realized the need for these rights, but she wanted to focus on the war and the POWs. She needed to help her son.

Min Lee could have read forever, but she suddenly realized that she needed to pick up Jim from his group and get home for lunch. She stopped at the desk to return her microfiche and questioned the librarian about getting an address of someone in Philadelphia. She hoped to write to Ethel Taylor personally and tell her about Mark. She didn't want her correspondence to get stuck in a pile of letters to the larger peace group itself.

"Simple!" replied the young librarian. "I could contact the library at Philly and ask them to check their city directory. Do you have her husband's name? Their address would be listed under his name, you know." Min Lee thought she seemed intrigued with the project.

"William Taylor. She's Ethel Barol Taylor. Obviously, from an affluent, maybe even prominent family. Her maiden name is mentioned in identifying her. If there is more than one William Taylor, I think she is about my age, around early fifties." Min Lee told the librarian.

"That will help. Give me a few days and check back."

Min Lee's heart felt less heavy as she hurried off to pick up Jim. She almost forgot that she would have to spend some time getting ready for her juniors and seniors who would be waiting for her in classes soon.

A week later, Min Lee thought she would check in at the library. The least she could do is give the librarian her telephone number, something she should have done when she made the request. She was barely inside the door of the microfiche room when she heard a hello that was too loud for a self-respecting librarian to project.

"Mrs. Gartley! I found the address you wanted! The Philly library got right back to me quickly," said the librarian as she walked toward Min Lee while waving a piece of paper that she handed to her when she was close enough.

"Thanks," Min Lee said as she peeked at the paper.

"Boy, she's an interesting lady! I hope it's okay with you that I looked her up and read a bit about her myself. Would you mind if I asked you what sort of project you are doing?"

Min Lee looked up at the librarian's eager face. "No, I don't mind at all. I'm researching groups that are questioning the war and are worried about Americans being held as prisoners in North Vietnam."

"Any special reason, ma'am?" The librarian looked at her with concern.

"Yes, my son Mark is a prisoner there."

"Mrs. Gartley, I'm so sorry. If there is anything I can do to help, you let me know, please."

"First of all, please call me Min Lee. I would love any help you could give me."

"I would enjoy doing some research for you. How old is Mark?"

"He's twenty-five now. He went missing in action over a year ago."

"He's my age, Min Lee."

"Thought as much, dear. I need to get home right now, but I'll be back soon. Thanks so much for the help."

CHAPTER 4

Getting Involved

September went by so fast it felt like a rug was being pulled out from beneath Min Lee's feet. She started teaching her history and civics classes at Dunedin High, enrolled Jim in a couple of community college courses that he didn't absolutely loathe, continued to research protest groups, and listened to Gerry's complaints about out-of-state bird hunters at the camp in Beaver Creek on economically brief, long distance phone calls.

As fast as the days sped by, the nights creeped along endlessly as Min Lee lay in bed and agonized about Mark. What were the conditions like at the prisoner of war camps? Was he getting enough to eat? How was he being treated by the North Vietnamese? She also mulled over and over again the idea of contacting Ethel Taylor. Getting involved in a peace group was a bit more daunting to her than she thought it would be.

Min Lee sat watching her class take a test in early October. Always a task master, she usually used a time like this to correct papers or make lesson plans, but she was lost in thought that day. The class she was observing was a senior group she found fun to work with. Curious and bright, they often pressed her with questions about current events as she tried to teach American History to them.

The students were worried about Vietnam and how it would affect their lives upon graduation, particularly the young men who would be draft bait if they didn't go on to college. How could she be truthful to them and tell them that she had questioned the purpose of this war even before her son Mark went off to fight in it? She knew it was not her place to share her political views with them. That was their parents' prerogative, but she couldn't help feeling protective of these students. They reminded her of Mark. They weren't much younger than him. Min Lee was overwhelmed with the feeling that she needed to do something about this situation. She had to become involved in something that would help her work toward a change in the policies keeping her Mark in a prisoner of war camp half way around the world. The bell rang to announce the end of the class period, and it woke Min Lee out of her deep reverie as students filed by her desk and stacked test papers on the edge of it.

That evening at home, Min Lee sat at her favorite spot. In her wicker rocking chair on her patio, she watched one of the beautiful sunsets for which Dunedin was famous. The sky looked like a piece of blown glass full of pinks, purples, and a tinge of orange. Plus, she enjoyed that magnificent, after dinner smoke. Jim was inside watching something foolish on television, so Min Lee could lose herself in thought as she had during the day without worry. She still had concerns about getting involved with some of these peace groups. She worried about the people she'd rub elbows with if she got involved. She took long drags on her cigarette and exhaled slowly. Suddenly, Mark's face filled her head. His seven month old face with large, hazel eyes as he nestled in the pack, she put him in, before hoisting it on her back that cold day in December, 1944. Wearing snowshoes, Min Lee trekked the two of them from the road, into the woods, and across a frozen cove to a point of land extending into Moosehead Lake. On this point there was a cabin where she would stay with Gerry. This spot was opposite the site of the Beaver Creek Camps she and Gerry would lease in 1945, buy in 1959 from the Hollingsworth and Whitney Paper Company, and operate in season for years.

After getting out of the army, Gerry had tried to work with Min Lee's widowed mother on the farm in Kentucky. Gerry and Mother Ligon did not see eye to eye, and Gerry took off for his home state of Maine. He wrote to Min Lee about coming to Beaver Creek if she wanted to stay with him. She packed up herself and baby Mark and went north. That move hadn't been easy, but she made it work. Min Lee made her decision about writing to Ethel Taylor of Women Strike for Peace.

She had faced challenges many times. As a new bride, Min Lee played mediator between her mother and Gerry before he left for Maine. She then coped with the prejudice from rural Mainers as she was a Southern girl. She didn't waste time debating with people. When questioned about what she believed concerning something specific, she usually said, "I'll have to think about that." She could deal with people of all walks of life. She would write to Ethel Taylor. That was that.

CHAPTER 5

Protesters vs Activists

In her research of organizations questioning the war over the next two months, Min Lee discovered what she considered to be a significant difference between protestors and actual activists, the latter being people who go out and do something other than shouting while holding signs. She also noted that there were peaceful activists and non-peaceful ones, to the point of violent activists, like the SDS, or Students for a Democratic Society. She read about the group called COLIAFAM, or Committee of Liaison with Families of Servicemen Detained in North Vietnam. This group was communicating with the North Vietnamese Women's Union, and they planned to meet with this group of women in Hanoi this December 1969 to try to start a letter exchange for the POWs. The meetings were called social get-togethers of these women's groups. Just women's business, of course. This intrigued Min Lee. How she longed to exchange letters with Mark!

Min Lee also scanned news of Joan Baez and her two sisters who were pictured on a poster. The poster had a slogan that read, "Girls say 'yes' to boys who say 'no.'" She loved Baez' songs but felt more comfortable with the

Women Strike for Peace slogan, "Not my son, not your son, not their sons."[1]

There were names mentioned of group members of some of the peace organizations that rather scared Min Lee, but she decided to take things one step at a time. She would write to Ethel Taylor in Philadelphia using the address that the young librarian had obtained for her. She would do it that evening after supper. Packing up her things to leave the library, Min Lee felt a positive rush for the first time in a long while.

That evening Min Lee hurried Jim through his supper. She uncharacteristically stacked the unwashed dishes in the sink and pulled out her writing stationery on the cleared table. With Jim plunked in front of the television, she started to write before she lost her nerve. Her worries about Mark poured out of her. She was surprised at how easy it was to introduce herself as the mother of a prisoner of war and talk about Mark to this woman she had never met. She told Ethel about the unconventional way she and her husband found out about Mark still being alive and in a prisoner of war camp. She added that she was questioning the war though she had been a supporter of the military when Mark's father was involved during World War II. Her letter sounded straightforward when she finished and reviewed it. Folding it and sticking it in the addressed envelope gave her a feeling of hope. Then, in rushed doubt about whether or not anything would come from this effort. She told herself either Ethel would answer or not. Fortunately, she had class lessons to work on and papers to grade as soon as she posted the letter. She absorbed herself in her work as she usually did to ignore the pangs of worry.

Two weeks went by quickly with Gerry arriving in Dunedin from Maine. He filled the mobile home with his presence and story upon story of camp dilemmas. A foolish bird hunter from Massachusetts had shot himself in the foot. Took him and the others in the hunting group forever to get him back to the jeep and into the hospital in Greenville. Also, he'd had trouble emptying the water pipes to close down camps, as he always did, thought Min Lee without saying a word. The mobile home seemed smaller now and would until Gerry started his winter job renting golf carts at the Belleview-Biltmore Hotel in nearby Bellaire. Min Lee was glad to dash off to school each morning. She had almost forgotten about Ethel Taylor until one afternoon upon returning home from classes, Gerry barked, "Who the hell do you know in Philadelphia, Min?"

"Where's the letter?" Min Lee threw her school bag down.

"On the counter. Since when do you have a friend in Philly?"

"Tell you in a minute, Gerry."

The address on the envelope was handwritten. Min Lee considered that a good sign. It wasn't some form letter from a secretary. She opened it with slightly shaky hands and her breath held. After reading the first couple lines, Min Lee released her breath and relaxed her tense shoulders. Ethel was actually thanking Min Lee for sharing her story about Mark. She encouraged her to continue communicating with their group Women Strike for Peace. Of most interest to her was the news that Ethel was part of the group that had been communicating with women in North Vietnam, and she and some of the American women planned to visit Hanoi just before this Christmas. They hoped they might be able to talk to some prisoners of war and exchange letters. Min Lee was astounded that this was actually going to happen.

Gerry was laughing at a television show with Jim, so Min Lee decided she would explain the letter later. She sat down at the table with a cigarette in one hand and a pen in the other and wrote back to Ethel. She gave Ethel extra details about her son and tried to impress on her how much it would mean to be able to hear from him in a letter. His father would be thrilled to hear from him as well, she wrote.

Min Lee posted the letter before she even gave a thought to making supper for the two Gartley men waiting for her to do so in the mobile home. Min Lee would tell Gerry what the letter from Philadelphia was all about while they ate. First though, she would relish her success at this first step to becoming involved with groups against the war by enjoying a cigarette on the mobile home's small patio. She grinned after blowing her first smoke ring. Her Mark felt a bit closer.

CHAPTER 6

Best Christmas Gift Ever

Life had a way of keeping Min Lee busy with school and the everyday routine. She felt grateful that she had work and family to keep her going and leave her little time to get lost in in the deep feeling of frustration about Mark's plight. She and Gerry were delighted to receive a clipping from a family who cut out the Bangor Dailey News article in the December 5th 1969 edition entitled *"Iron Curtain Photo, Warm Hearts –Tell Family Missing Son is a POW."*[1]

Journalist Ken Buckley received a tip about the Gartleys finding out about Mark in such an unusual way. He interviewed Gerry in Greenville before Gerry left for Dunedin. Buckley wrote about how the Gartleys had received the magazine photo and letter from the Polish couple and had not received an official word from the military. This was the first notice of Mark's capture in a newspaper. Buckley quoted Gerry as describing Mark as "the young lad running around the dooryard up to the camp, among the people who came to hunt and fish the northern wilderness." This charming mention of the Beaver Creek Camps made Min Lee smile.[2]

News in the first part of December was full of Nixon's start of the military draft lottery. It was the first time the United States had used this since World War II. Min Lee was worried that this could mean more military aggression on the country's part in Southeast Asia. The second half of the month arrived with its usual tasks for Christmas preparation. In snowless Dunedin, Min Lee felt it especially important to make their mobile home look festive. With each decoration that went up, though, thoughts of Ethel Taylor and her companions going to North Vietnam appeared in Min Lee's head. She worried about them and their safety. She wondered if they would be able to make contact with Mark. Gerry warned her about getting her hopes up too high.

"Min, the situation over there is very delicate. Lord only knows what those women will find when they get to Hanoi." Gerry was drinking a cup of coffee and watching his wife wrestle with a string of lights for the front of the mobile home.

"Why is it we always put these damned things away in a hurry without any thought as to how difficult it will be to deal with them the next Christmas? Who wrapped these lights so haphazardly, anyway?" fussed Min Lee.

Her husband didn't answer her soon enough, and she threw the entire, beach ball-sized mass of lights up in the air. The thud created by their landing on the linoleum floor of the kitchen caught Gerry's attention.

"Min, who cares about a string of Christmas lights?" Gerry put his cup down and gave her a concerned look.

"How do you think they'll find Mark?" Min asked. "Behind enemy lines and all."

"I have no idea, Min."

"Gerry, it's the 16th. Should we have heard from them by now?"

As Min Lee and Gerry looked down at the Christmas lights, the phone rang. Jim got to it first and hollered out, "Aunt Josephine is on the phone from Bangor. All riled up! Something about a George Hale."

"What?" both Gerry and Min Lee uttered almost together. Jim was back in front of the television after balancing the phone receiver on the kitchen counter. Min Lee picked it up. "Josephine?" she said into the phone. "What's up?"

"Oh, my God, Min Lee, oh, my God! I was watching WABI news, and they started talking about a women's group visiting North Vietnam. Well, I just thought it was the usual bunch of peaceniks, and I wasn't paying much attention until suddenly I heard his voice, Min Lee."

"Whose voice, Josephine?"

"His voice, Min Lee! Mark's!"

Min Lee dropped the receiver and hugged herself. Gerry leaned down and picked it up. "Josephine? What the hell are you going on about?"

"Gerry, I heard a recording of Mark's voice. It was him! I'm sure!"

"Josephine, speak up loud. I'm going to hold the receiver out for Min to hear. What did he say?" Gerry stretched his arm holding the receiver out toward Min Lee.

"He said 'make the eggnog extra strong.'[3] And he also mentioned 'Merry Christmas' and 'tell Jim to do well in school.'"[4] Josephine was out of breathe from yelling and gasped a couple times.

Gerry and Min Lee stood speechless with the phone receiver between them.

"Gerry? Min Lee? Are you folks still there?"

"Yes, Josephine." Gerry said in a long exhale.

"What?"

"We're here, Josephine," remarked Min Lee. "It's such a wonderful surprise. We knew about the trip the women were making, but we didn't know if they would be able to find Mark. This is phenomenal."

"Well, I have called the television station, you know our Chanel 5 up here that we watch for the news and all. George Hale, remember his name? One of the reporters. He assures me he can get a recording that I can play for you over the phone. Then you can hear him for yourselves. Will also send it down, so you can play it as many times as you want to. How's that, huh?"

"Oh, Josephine, that will be the best Christmas gift ever!" said Min Lee. "Thanks!"

"Gotta run! These calls all the way to Florida get expensive. Love you all!"

"Bye!" both Gerry and Min Lee said. Still holding the receiver, Gerry looked at Min Lee.

"Guess they found our boy, Min."

"Thank God, they did, Gerry."

They looked sideways to find Jim grinning at them from the other end of the counter. The Christmas lights did not get put up until the next day.

CHAPTER 7

In the News

As January of 1970 arrived, Min Lee and Gerry either found or received several different newspaper articles about the contact made with Mark and two other POWs. The articles spanned the past month of the Women Strike for Peace trip to Vietnam and the reaction it received in the United States. An AP story circulated accompanied by a picture of Mark, along with another pilot Paul Bordon Brown of Newton, Massachusetts, and Bill Mayhew of New Manchester, West Virginia. Bill was the navigator and only crewman abroad Mark's plane. Mrs. Madeline Duckles of Berkeley, California, a leader of the Committee of Responsibility and a member of the Women's International League for Peace and Freedom, and Mrs. Cora Weiss of New York, a national coordinator of Women Strike for Peace were in one of the photographs with the three POWs. Min would find out later from Ethel Taylor that Ethel made the trip, too, but became sick and went home before the actual meeting with the POWs. The women had been invited to visit by the Women's Union of Vietnam. It was at this time that a monthly exchange of letters and an increase weight and frequency of packages was arranged. When the women left Hanoi, they carried the first significant number of letters, which were sealed. The Committee of Liaison with Families of Servicemen Detained in North Vietnam or COLIAFAM, of which Cora was co-chair, immediately mailed the letters to whomever they were addressed. That committee continued to send three people from the United States to Vietnam every month carrying mail by hand to and from Hanoi.[1]

The Record American from Boston, Massachusetts, ran a story on December 24, 1969, headlining their native son Paul Bordon Brown with bold letters announcing *"Newton Pilot, POW Since 1968, Alive."* The article told a poignant story of Brown's mother receiving a letter from her son that started with "Dear Mom and Dad." She wept upon reading this as her husband, Paul's father, had died a year ago at Christmas time. News that the pilots were feeling fine was also noted, and names of other families receiving letters from POWs was shared. [2] Min Lee lingered over this story one Sunday afternoon as she and Gerry had many articles spread across the coffee table.

"Gerry, sometimes I feel frustrated about the whole POW situation, but imagine how this dear woman felt upon finally receiving news from her son after losing her husband. It's heartbreaking." Min shook her head.

"Better than losing both of them, Min." Gerry reached around Min to grab another article. "Is this the Bangor one? Want to peek more carefully at what my young buddy Ken Buckley wrote about the latest developments."

Maine newspapers, of course, focused on Mark with headlines like *"Hanoi Airs Maine Flier's Greeting"* and *"Aunt Knows Nephew's Greetings." The Bangor Daily News* [3] in Maine ran an article that recounted the story of how the Gartleys heard from Gerry's sister Josephine about the recording of the POWs that included Mark's voice. It reported that Aunt Josephine was surprised but positive the voice on the tape was her brother's son. She is quoted in the article as saying, "To me it's something you read in fiction–it doesn't happen in real life. But it happened here." [4]

This particular article also explained further about the Polish magazine article the Gartleys had received in August of 1969. Polish writer Monika Warenska did a tour of North Vietnam and interviewed a group of POWs that included Lieutenant Mark Gartley. Warenska described the POW camps as austere, but she also said Gartley was not seriously injured and endearingly called him "a blue-eyed blond."

"What I can't figure, Min, is how the newspapers now know about this Polish article and its author. Even named her. Why wouldn't the military contact us about it?" Gerry held the article in his hand and looked it over several times as if somehow the answer to his question would suddenly appear.

"Makes you pause, doesn't it," replied Min.

The Portland Press Herald ran a story about the three American women going to Hanoi, and as Ethel Taylor developed a sinus infection and returned home, only two were there to meet the POWs. They related that the women brought letters from the POWs revealing 132 names of men being held in the camps, some of whom had been missing for two to three years. One letter was from Mark. The news of the deaths of five men who had been missing was also shared. The article reported that Weiss and Duckles said the three POWs they met with seemed in good condition. They "drank beer happily." [5] The women told reporters they had mailed letters from POWs Sunday from Philadelphia upon their return.

"Some of these newspapers that only did interviews over the telephone got details wrong, didn't they?" Min said. "I suppose just getting the word out about POWs and MIAs is better than not, even with some inaccuracies."

Gerry simply grunted in agreement. He scanned another article.

Min Lee and Gerry spent hours poring over all the articles and a letter from Mark brought back by the peace group, but their favorite thing to do was to listen to the tape of Mark's voice that Josephine had sent. Min had been interviewed by the *St. Petersburg Times* and the *Clearwater Sun* in December. She explained to both reporters that she was certain the voice on the tape was her son Mark. He had studied Speech at Georgia Tech, so he had a clear voice.

Gerry scolded Min Lee about wearing the tape completely out by rewinding and playing it again and again, so they were surprised and thrilled to receive a package from the American Broadcasting Company in New York at the end of January. It contained a new tape and a letter from Tom O'Brien, the vice president and director of radio news at ABC.

Mr. O'Brien explained that they had received a copy of the audio tape from their bureau in Moscow. They had broadcast it. ABC wanted the Gartleys to have a copy as they thought it would be a clearer copy of the interview of the POWs than what might have been taped on home devices.

Minnie smiled broadly as she read the ending of the letter aloud to Gerry and Jim. "All of us join in hoping that we will be able to broadcast word of Lt. Gartley's release as soon as is humanly possible. Sincerely, Tom O'Brien." [6]

"Thank God," said Gerry. "The scratches in the old tape are becoming louder than the voices." He tilted his head back with a huge grin on his face.

CHAPTER 8

The D.C. Convention

Corresponding with Ethel Taylor in the next few months gave Min Lee a chance to get to know these women who were working toward the goal of getting POWs out of North Vietnam and ending the war. She was intrigued that they possibly paid their own way to meet with some of the prisoners with the aid of the North Vietnamese Women's Union and to start the letter swap. They were obviously women of means to do what they wanted to do, but she was still impressed that they chose to get involved in the peace movement. Min Lee also started hearing from other mothers of POWs after being in the newspapers. She really enjoyed finding other POW mothers in Florida.

In April, the Gartleys received a copy of a notice in *The Dragon's Tale*, a Beta Theta Pi publication at the Georgia Tech Institute of Technology where Mark had done his undergraduate degree, in 1966. It reported Mark's status as a POW. It also listed Min's address in Dunedin and encouraged fellow Beta friends to write message of interest and concern to her. A classmate Pete Cockey had been in touch with Min Lee, and he said she didn't want any condolences but would appreciate letters. [1]

Min Lee decided to become involved in the National League of Families of American Prisoners in Southeast Asia. It worried her that North Vietnam did not abide by the Geneva Convention in regard to the treatment of prisoners of war. She also found out that there was concern about Americans taken prisoner in Laos or South Vietnam.

"Listen to the objectives of this group, Gerry. I think you'll agree this is a good organization," said Min Lee to her husband over the supper table upon finishing their meal one evening. The first is to secure humane treatment for POWs as outlined in the Geneva Convention and recognized by general humanitarian standards. Who could object to that?

"No one I know, Min."

"Next is to stimulate continuing world concern about the fate of the men and the plight of their families."

"Ayuh, what else?"

"This one is something that really needs to be worked on, Gerry. The third objective is to improve dissemination of the information concerning the POW-MIA problem not only to the press and to families of the captured and missing men, but to agencies of the government.[2] Gerry, there is no excuse for families not finding out sooner about their missing men." Min Lee held the brochure she had been reading from and scanned it once more silently.

"Is this group anti-war, Min?"

"No, they aren't. They don't take a side on that issue. It says here somewhere that they want to get everyone's backing regardless of their stand on the war's legitimacy. All people can unite about the prisoner of war issue. I think that's smart for right now. Don't you?"

"I guess so, but if they don't protest the war, what are they going to do to be heard?"

"Well, it says the League urges all citizens to write in behalf of prisoners to their senators and representatives. Do you think they can have an impact?"

"Hard telling, Min. Worth a shot, I guess."

In May after Gerry had left for Beaver Creek, Min Lee was invited to attend the Appeal for International Justice for American POWs and MIAs at the DAR Convention Hall in Washington, D.C. It would be her first official taste of politics nationally as a representative of the League she had joined. She was pleased to get Friday off from teaching to fly up for the opening meeting scheduled that evening at 8pm. She wondered if the school administration enjoyed her being a bit of a celebrity in the area after all the press at Christmas time. The weekend proved to be an overwhelming affair. She typed a letter to Gerry, who had left for Maine, with all the details that Sunday night when she got back to Dunedin.

"Dear Gerry: I thought perhaps you might have been calling just now as the telephone rang and it sounded like it might have been a long-distance wire open but no voices at all. Telephone calls have been messed up lately, I get wrong numbers or nothing often, must be something wrong.

Well, it was quite a day and night at Washington. They finally decided we could go at such a late date I couldn't go from McDill and found a flight coming in to take families from McCoy Base at Orlando. There was calling back and forth from me to St. Pete, to Washington, to me for two days. And then from me to McDill, to McCoy and from them to me and St. Pete. You remember how the telephone rang at Christmas, and it was going on at school too. Anyhow finally they agreed that they could get my authorization through at Washington and down to McCoy and would be waiting for me. I was to get there at 9 to leave at 10. Said that an Air National Guard plane was coming in with 62 aboard to pick us up there. Seems the Air Guard had agreed to put on flights all over the country. Well I got there early (imagine that?) and ate breakfast with the pilot – an ex W.War II fighter pilot. There were in there with a huge Air Guard that seated about 90. There were 8 there to go. There was no one on it as it was sent from Penn. Just to pick us up. Snafu!! Seems that all those who knew they were going (dependents) had already arranged to go to Patrick Air Base at the Cape and go from there, and those of us who were there had been notified at the last minute of this flight. Many did not know about it and couldn't go, I'm sure. Mary Doak would certainly have liked to have gone, and the Col. told me that I wouldn't have needed authorization, that he would have taken me without it.

We left at 10:30. As it was a 4-engine old propeller plane, it didn't go too fast but we got to Washington Andrews Air Force Base at 2:30. Military busses took us to the Sheraton-Park in Washington. I registered and got a sandwich and got acquainted with a mother and a wife from Houston. Since I was alone I went with them from then on.

One thing about this meeting – there were over 1000 there – was that everybody was there for the same purpose, everybody wanted to hear your story and your wanted to hear theirs. That is all the talk was about, and it seemed good to talk with people who really cared and understood what you were talking about.

We were bussed to the Rayburn Office building (a huge building for the offices of the House of Rep.) but went into a fairly small basement long hall and room for a buffet put on by Fairchild Hiller Corp. I guess they didn't expect as many. People were crowded closer than I was ever in a crowd, most could not even get to the few tables which had a little sliced meat and buns and some punch. It was terribly hot, and in this crowd suddenly I was beside Senator Dole who sponsored and pushed for the affair. I talked with him a little, looked around and right against my shoulder was Sec. Defense Laird shaking hands with the women. I am most sorry that as I shook his hand and talked a moment, I was too surprised, hot, tired and hungry to do anything but cry. I had something to say to him, that I could have said if I had had any idea that I would have had a chance. The press was following him and Sec. State Rogers and General James who along with Senator Dole spoke in that hot, crowded place. Ross Perot was there talking with someone but I did not see him there.

Then we were bussed to Constitution Hall, and all this 1000 or more went in together and filled most of the main floor auditorium I think. It really was a very inspirational meeting. I think highly of Senator Dole – more that of any of the politicians I've met. Very unassuming and very sincere. Is a disabled veteran I think – has one arm he doesn't use. Those who spoke there were Sen. Dole (he named the congressmen who were in the audience- none from Maine tho Muskie's name was on the program as one of the sponsors. I asked Sen. Dole when I talked with him at the Rayburn Bldg. if Sen Muskie would be there, and he said he didn't know, that he hoped so.

Senator Goldwater gave them hell, and us a very good pep talk.

Mayor of Washington, Mrs. Stockdale (the woman from California League of families), some other POW wives, a congressman from Florida, Robert Cummings (from Hollywood), Lt. Frishman and Hegdahl both spoke briefly to do all we could and keep on in behalf of our men, the H. Ross Perot got right down to things he thought should be done that he had told the Senate Foreign Relations Com. That afternoon in briefing session on POWs (he had concrete suggestions), then Captain James Lovell (the Apollo 13 pilot), then the surprise guest who came in and spoke very well was Spiro Agnew. Gen James also spoke.

When we got back to the hotel about 11:45, many hadn't eaten all day and there was absolutely nothing you could get to eat in the whole huge hotel unless it was peanuts and beer at the bar. All too tired to do that. I moved in with the woman from Houston and let Mary Ann Fuller from Jacksonville and her daughter have my room.

Next morning we went to Dept. of Interior for a very disappointing meeting of just the families. Mrs. Stockdale not a good organizer and with so many of those there knowing nothing about this – some have recently found themselves in the middle of it and don't know like those of us who have been in it longer – these were anxious to find out something and what they could do and it was time to leave before much was really done (too many kudos given to those who had done this or that.) I talked with so many who have army men and air force down in S. Vietnam and Laos and of course all are listed as missing and no hope of news and too much emphasis given POWs to suit them, and I could not help but agree that pressure should be put on those in gov't to release names too.

Back to hotel and bussed to Andrews again. I had gotten to bed at 1:30 and the woman from Texas hadn't slept and was up at 4:30 and we went looking for some place for coffee at 6 that morning. We waited at Andrews until the last flight to go and 12 going from there. Then we took off about 4. We took those from Savannah, Ga., dropped them and then off for Maxwell Air Force Base in Alabama, the finally arrived at Orlando at 11pm. I don't believe I was ever as tired. My age and lack of sleep and food had caught up with me. If there had not been a couple from Tarpon Springs along who followed me across the state I would not have attempted to drive home. As it was I just made it mile by mile and wondered if I could make the next. Of course I'm glad I went, but again we were disappointed because the press did not cover it nationally. Nothing in our local papers and that was the whole purpose - to get the attention of the people." [3]

Jim was looking at his mother from across the living room when Min looked up from her typewriter. He smiled.

"Jim, I had to get it all down on paper to remember all the details. And I know your dad would be interested in what went on up there this weekend. How about going out for a burger, and I'll fill you in on the highlights as we eat?"

"Sounds good, Mom."

Later that evening as Min Lee got ready for school on Monday, she wondered where all this would take her. At least she was trying to do something, she told herself, but she had that familiar ache again. Half heart ache, half desperation. It was deep and intolerable at quiet moments. Tonight, it took her back to 1943 when she heard that her first husband had been shot down over the Solomon Islands during a raid over Rekata Bay during World War II. The dreadful feeling of "why him, dammit." Her sweet C.C.!

Min Lee became Mrs. Charles Cedar Hughes in July of 1937 in Mayfield, Kentucky. They were both 21 years old and had different goals. They divorced the following September of 1938, but they exchanged letters long after that. C.C. wrote love letters to Min Lee from wherever he was stationed, called her angel face, and pleaded with her to wait for him. One of C.C.'s letters had ended with "...and don't sit under the apple tree with anyone else but me."[4]

Min Lee knew C.C. wanted to get back together with her after the war, but she met and became involved with Gerry at Fort Knox. She was newly married to Gerry by the time she received word of what had happened to C.C. in the Pacific theater, but she kept his letters, along with his picture, their marriage certificate, divorce degree, and a Kentucky newspaper clipping telling of his death. She stored them all in a carved wooden box. She still had it all these years later. When Mark announced that he was going to train to be a fighter pilot, all Min Lee could think of was just like her C.C. Sometimes it was almost too much to bear.

CHAPTER 9

Summer in Maine

The school year of 1969-1970 came to a close, and Min Lee was faced with the task of packing for the trip back up to Maine. As she stacked clean clothes on her bed and tried to remember what she had left in Beaver Creek and what she still needed to pack, she thought about her last conversation with a male student. He had confided to her that he was not going to college. He was going to sign up for the Marines.

"Might as well be the best, Mrs. Gartley. I've always admired Marines." The student's face took on a handsome, full-face smile.

"I suppose that's right." Min Lee smiled back in support.

"Oh, no offense about your son. Pilots are admirable, too. But you need a college degree to fly. I'm too impatient for that right now."

"No offense taken. Please be careful, though."

"Do you hear from your son?"

"Some, but not enough. I guess he is doing okay."

They heard voices coming from down the hall.

"That would be my buddies! Gotta go! Enjoyed your class this year, Mrs.

Gartley. Bye!"

"Take care." Min Lee started to wave but noticed he was out the classroom door without looking back. She was left with a feeling of anxiety for yet another young man.

The journey back to Beaver Creek was uneventful. With Min Lee's "lead foot" as Gerry called it, they made record time. Min Lee and Jim were becoming accustomed to the drive and knew good places to stop for meals and lodging. When they arrived, Maine was a beautiful relief with its crisp, late spring weather—cool nights, warm but not hot days, and low humidity, especially compared to Florida the first of June. This move seemed easier to Min Lee as she set about settling herself and Jim into camp life. There was a strong sense of comfort knowing that her Mark was alive and seemed to be coping with being a prisoner in North Vietnam. She also looked forward to doing some work in Maine for the League of POW families she had joined.

June had almost melted into July when the Gartleys received word about Mark being on a television show emceed by Walter Cronkite. He was to appear in a documentary made by a Swedish film crew in Hanoi. The film would be in a question-and-answer format. A fifteen page transcript would be made available, too. The Gartleys learned from the Swedish Ambassador that Mark and his wingman, or navigator Bill Mayhew had been taken to downtown Hanoi. There they were interviewed by several North Vietnamese Army officials for the benefit of the film crew. They also received word from one of Cronkite's agents that they would be sent the section of the film which featured Mark. Min notified Bill's parents Mr. and Mrs. Stewart Mayhew of the upcoming television show.

The Mayhews watched from their West Virginia home. Mrs. Mayhew was quoted in their local newspaper saying that her Bill "looked very, very good to me." She also shared that they were able to get letters to him and from him, plus six and one-half pound packages with things such as vitamins, soap, candy, and pictures of the family. [1]

Min Lee and Gerry were excited to see their son on television. He was interviewed by a Swedish woman by the name of Ingrid Dahlberg who informed the audience "that while the airmen were not told by the North

Vietnamese just what to say…it was obvious that they did not want their remarks to be of such a nature as to produce an unfavorable reaction toward them or their fellow prisoners." [2]

Min Lee gave Gerry a concerned look upon hearing that comment, but they had no time to voice their feelings as Mark appeared on the screen and said, "My treatment has been very good ever since I got…since I was captured. It's been much better than I'd ever…than I'd expect it to be, and we look at the country as, as it's been bombed by our aircraft, and it is a poor country materially in goods. The standard in which we are kept is very good. It's very good." [3] Cronkite closed the interview clip with a few comments. Gerry signaled for their son Jim to turn off the television.

"He looks good, Min." Gerry glanced at his wife. She was quiet for a moment.

"How much do you think the North Vietnamese prompted him in his comments, Gerry?"

"Hard telling. He didn't seem to be speaking freely, did he?"

"No, he didn't." Min Lee rubbed at her face with both hands.

"This business isn't easy, you know." Gerry leaned into Min Lee.

"I know! I know!" Min Lee rubbed her thighs and jumped up from the couch. "Dinner won't make itself."

"Min?"

"I'm okay, Gerry," said Min Lee as she walked toward the kitchen.

"Right," said Gerry as he shook his head and looked at Jim. Jim shrugged his shoulders.

In an interview with Ken Buckley of the Bangor Daily News a few days later, Gerry voiced concerns about why Mark was receiving so much attention from the North Vietnamese. Buckley quoted him in the paper as saying, "I don't know what the idea is behind so much publicity. There are so many other prisoners in North Vietnam and I'm wondering why he gets so much." [4]

Gerry also told the reporter that they were now receiving regular mail from Mark. The letters were censored, but in them Mark reassured his family that he was doing fine. He had also received the packages his parents sent him. The news from him and pictures they had seen had comforted the Gartleys, but they were left wondering why the news of his captivity did not match up with what other released POWs. Doug Hegdahl, who had been released, had described mistreatment of prisoners. Gerry did tell Buckley "I don't think they (the North Vietnamese) told him to say anything and he (Mark) said it." [5] Gerry also told Buckley that he did not feel his son would spread propaganda for the enemy.

Upon reading the article in the Bangor Daily a few evenings after the interview, Min Lee lowered her paper and spoke to Gerry who was busy untangling fishing lures. "There's some strong suggestion in this piece."

"Of what?"

"Of Mark being used by the North Vietnamese even though you said you felt he wasn't."

"Well, that concern was brought up by me, Min, not Ken. That young Ken is all right."

"I guess. He did say you voiced the concerns here."

"Is it too much, Min? Should I stop speaking to Ken?"

"No, according to the League of families, any publicity about the POWs is good. Makes you realize we are walking a fine line here, though, doesn't it?"

The summer passed quickly. Min Lee tried to share with friends and acquaintances in the Greenville area the importance of writing to the congressmen from Maine about the issue of the POW/MIAs. She had the names of Senators Smith and Muskie, and Representatives Kyros and Hathaway, along with addresses, on the tip of her tongue to offer up to anyone who seemed interested in the mailing campaign, but she found mostly sympathetic ears about Mark's plight yet deaf ears about becoming involved in actually contacting people in government. In fact, she was surprised to often find a great reluctance to get involved.

"I guess the expression 'it depends on whose tail is caught in the door' is true, Gerry," she fumed one night at supper. "Everyone feels sorry for the prisoners, but no one wants to do anything."

"You can't force people to become politically involved, Min," Gerry replied. "A lot of folks don't want to stick their noses in when it comes to government stuff."

"Well, then how will this write-in campaign ever do any good?"

"Takes time, Min."

"We don't have a lot of time, Gerry. How long do you want those men to stay in those camps? How long can our Mark withstand whatever it is that he has to tolerate to stay alive?"

"Min, you can only do as much as you can do, is all I'm saying. I admire what you're trying to do here, but you have to accept the fact that not everyone will be willing to get involved in these things. Min, do you understand what I'm trying to say?"

"Hmm."

Supper was finished in silence that evening.

A chilly nip greeted them one morning soon after that, and it was time for Min Lee and Jim to pack for Dunedin for another school year. Mark had been a POW for two years now—one in which they didn't know if he was dead or alive and now one in which they anguished about his treatment in a prisoner of war camp. Min Lee felt she needed to do more.

CHAPTER 10

Trinkets to Tug at Heart Strings

School started as efficiently as usual that fall of 1970, but Min Lee felt unsettled as she sat at her desk after school one day and doodled on her lesson plan book—something she never did. Some days she felt like she'd gained a lot in the past year with news of Mark, even hearing his voice and seeing him on television. But other days like today, she felt as if she was getting nowhere. She decided she needed to reach out to her friends at the League of Families and see what was new when she got home.

"So glad you called, Min Lee!" a League friend almost sang into the phone. "We just received a package from California. Can't wait to share this with you!"

"Okay, you have my attention. What is in the package?"

"Bracelets!"

"What in the world?'

"Min Lee, bracelets with POW's or MIA's names, ranks, and the dates they went missing engraved on them. We've been asked to help sell them."

Min Lee grinned into the phone receiver. "What an idea! Who did this?"

"A group called VIVA which stands for Voices in Vital America. [1] They're college students who wanted to do something concrete for the effort. They want us to sell them for $2.50 to $3.00. The people who buy them are told to wear them until the POW or MIA on their particular bracelet is found or he has returned home. Come on over and get some and read their information brochure. It's amazing. They actually have the big celebrities Bob Hope and Martha Raye as honorary chairs."

When Min Lee got home after picking up some of the bracelets, she opened the package and read the information about them. Television personality and Congressman Bob Dornan had gotten a bracelet like these while in Vietnam. After lots of effort, this VIVA group had received a donation of enough brass and copper to make 1200 bracelets. The brass ones would be sold for $2.50. The copper bracelets would be advertised as good for people with tennis elbow and sold for an extra fifty cents or $3.00. VIVA planned to make many more bracelets, as well as bumper stickers, buttons, and cards. Min Lee found out that a big business was planning to help the League with Christmas cards.

Min Lee thought this was just what was needed to make their efforts more visible. These bracelets would be the perfect conversation starters as people noticed them on friends' and relatives' wrists. She was also intrigued by the greeting card idea. Christmas would be upon them in no time. She asked someone about them at the next League meeting she attended and found out they were being printed as they spoke.

Fairchild Hiller Corporation, a business involved in aviation and printing, in collaboration with the League of Families of POW/MIAs, led by its president Mrs. James B. Stockdale, planned to supply Christmas cards to League members to send to friends and politicians that encouraged everyone to contact world leaders to urge North Vietnam to honor the Geneva Convention and end abuse of war prisoners. [2]

Later when the cards came, Min was somewhat taken aback at first by the solemn appearance of them. Simple gold with some red and the caption that read "Pray for them," along with a picture of a pilot in full gear and then a POW in dismal, Spartan surroundings. On the back of the card was a serious message about writing to United Nations delegates who might have influence on North Vietnam and take them to task about not following the rules of the Geneva Convention concerning their treatment of prisoners of war. Listed were the names of delegates from USSR, Sweden, Romania, and Poland. The Polish delegate Stefan Jedrychowski caught Min Lee's eye. She had been unaware of these countries' opinions of the United States intervention in Vietnam. They didn't approve of the United States being in Vietnam. She fretted about all she didn't know about all these political ins and outs for a minute then decided to sit down and write a list of card recipients.

The League also distributed stickers for inserting into the cards for recipients to use as they saw fit. Some read "Pray for your prisoners-Don't let them be forgotten-They won't be home for Christmas!" Or "Remember our Prisoners of War-They won't be home for Christmas." Min Lee particularly liked the ones with a tiny image of a POW, Lieutenant Commander Richard Allen Stratton and the reading "Silent Nights-Lest we forget- POW-MIA." Christmas preparations would be concerned with promoting the idea for more concern for the POW/MIAs and less worry about gifts and decorations.

A month later in their Dunedin mobile home, Min Lee had an assembly line set up at the kitchen table. She was writing names and addresses on envelopes, Jim was stuffing them with cards, and Gerry, who had arrived at Dunedin after hunting season and closing down the camp in Maine, was wetting stamps on a sponge and placing them on the envelopes.

"I need a break!" Gerry announced as he shoved the dish with the sponge in it across the table.

"We have a lot more to go," Min Lee said without breaking her pace at writing.

"My fingers are sticky and soggy, 'Teach.'"

Jim laughed. "The Odd Couple is on in ten minutes."

"Perfect! Turn it on, Son."

"Okay, one episode and then I really need your help again."

"Yes," both father and son said as one went to the television and the other went to the cupboards in search of a snack.

"Take a minute off with us, Min," pleaded Gerry with a bag of chips in his hands. "You like this show."

Min Lee sat at the table for a few seconds and scowled their way and then gave up and went to take a seat with them. A laugh might do me good, she decided.

CHAPTER 11

Son Tay

The Gartleys sat at their Thanksgiving table in late November. Everything was perfectly laid out in front of them. Gerry's requested rolls. Jim's perennially favorite cranberry sauce. Even a custard pie sat waiting on the kitchen counter. Min Lee made it just for herself as no one else liked it. There was no usual holiday cheer, though. Min Lee's bad mood loomed over her husband and son.

"What was so wrong with their intelligence that they raided an empty facility? That's what I'd like to know." Min Lee sat in front of the uncarved turkey with her hands flat on the table, one on either side of her empty plate.

The Gartleys had received word about the failed prisoner of war raid on the town of Son Tay, which was twenty-three miles west of North Vietnam's capital city. Starting in May of 1970, United States intelligence was taking aerial photographs of the POW camp that held up to 60 prisoners. They even felt that the prisoners were attempting to send signals to them. On November 21, Secretary of Defense Melvin Laird had ordered the raid carried out by American Green Berets to rescue the prisoners. According to the military, the operation was perfectly executed with not one life lost. Unfortunately, the prisoners' quarters were found empty. Prisoners had been moved to a different location. Some League members considered it a grand failure of the government. Some felt that at least it showed the government's commitment to not forget the POWs. The whole affair upset Min Lee. [1]

"We don't really know what happened, Min," Gerry said. "These things aren't easy."

"Two years and three months, Gerry." Min Lee made no move to start serving their dinner.

They sat in silence for a few minutes. Jim said nothing as he looked from his mother to his father. "Shall we eat this later?" asked Gerry.

"Carve the turkey, Gerry." Min Lee sat like a statue as Gerry and Jim made small talk and served up the Thanksgiving bird and the fixings. Gerry cautiously put small servings of food on Min's plate. She sat for the next hour moving food around on her plate without a morsel making it to her mouth. She didn't taste her pie either.

Later that week, a Christmas card initially sent to Greenville Maine, made its way to Dunedin. With the White House in a gold seal on the front of the card, the message inside read,

"With our sincere wishes for a joyous Christmas and a Happy New Year. The President and Mrs. Nixon."

"How ironic and insensitive at this time!" Min Lee frowned at it before tossing it on the coffee table.

CHAPTER 12

Christmas 1970

Min Lee's heart lightened somewhat the next week when on December 2, NBC-TV news broadcast from Radio Hanoi a message from Mark. In it he said the following:

"As the holidays approach once more, my thoughts center on past Christmases and delight in creating Christmases that might have been and that yet will be.

My Christmas spirit is not limited by space or time, but travels around the globe to be with you again this year. As you celebrate I will be merry. When you sing carols, I will hear. As you enjoy the Christmas treats, I will be satisfied. But if you are sad, then I will be blue.

Be merry this Christmas and don't worry about me or my welfare. I am in good health and receiving good treatment during my detention here. Many efforts are being made to make each Christmas better than its predecessor.

I have roommates and we play basketball and volleyball each day. We also have a small garden. I am receiving your letters and photos.

We are able to receive more packages now. Check latest instructions for timing and articles. This Christmas we can receive an 11-pound package. Less sweets and more durable, useful or tasty articles would be nice.

Merry Christmas to all my relatives and friends. May all our lives be enriched by feelings of peace, honor, good will towards men.

Love, Mark." [1]

The Gartleys all tried to enjoy Christmas when it arrived for Mark's sake. Even Min Lee tried to be merry as she planned what she would say two days later when a national NBC television crew was scheduled to arrive and interview her. She decided if Mark could be upbeat from North Vietnam, she could as well. After the Christmas gift exchanges, she sat down to write and rewrite what she would say to the camera. She even wrote it in holiday red ink:

This is the third Xmas Mark has been in a North Vietnamese prison. When Nixon offered to exchange prisoners we hoped that they would be home with their families. This past year we have received letters for the first time and have been able to send a 6 ½ pound package for Christmas. Mark's last letter was written in October, and I know he has been given some of his packages this year, and he had received three letters and his 1969 Christmas cards.

I feel that the increase in communication with the prisoners and the increased numbers of men who have been identified and have been allowed to write has been largely a result of the wonderful response of the thousands of Americans who wrote letters and offered prayers in their behalf, and as a mother of a prisoner, I want to take this opportunity to thank all of them.

My heart is sad for the families of over 1,000 American boys who are listed as missing-in-action who live in daily hope that they will hear some news of their loved ones. If this year those same wonderful American people will also write to the Lao Patriot Front, Vientiane Lao, and to Madame Vinh, National Liberation Front, Paris Peace Talks, Paris and ask that they observe the Geneva Agreements concerning the treatment of the prisoners of war.

But most of all, I pray that before another Christmas the war is over and all Americans in Southeast Asia, prisoners and American troops, are at home. [2]

"Very well put!" announced Gerry as he, Min Lee, and Jim watched Min Lee's interview on television later that week.

"I don't mind speaking in front of a class or any group of people live, but that television camera bothered me, I'm afraid. Did you two really think it was okay?" Min Lee still sat rigid in her chair as she had while watching the television.

"It was good!" Jim said.

"When did you not sound good, my dear," Gerry said with a tweak of Min Lee's left shoulder. "What's for desert since we missed it to turn on the news?"

"So much for my moment of glory, huh?"

"Mother Gartley used to say 'life goes around like a button on a backhouse door.'" Gerry winked at Min Lee now.

"Yuck!" Jim said, and both his parents laughed.

Min Lee also did an interview with the local Pinellas Mobile Home Association newsletter that month. The article reiterated in print Mark's Christmas message as heard on the NBC program, ran a brief bio of Mark, interviewed his mother briefly, and shared this message and request from her:

"'Message to You

The families of the Missing-in-Action and Prisoners–of–War in Southeast Asia did not begin to speak out and to publicize the terrible plight of their brave sons and husbands until 1969, though many American boys had already been missing or prisoners for as long as five years.

Now, a year later, I believe most Americans are conscious of them. And I believe it has been the thousands of letters written to the officials of North Vietnam and to other countries which have caused the North Vietnamese to release more names of men they hold as names of some of those who have died in prison, and to allow more prisoners to write and receive letters occasionally, and to allow families to send a 6-lb., 6-oz. package every other month. This has been a comfort to some families, but there are over 900 families who have heard nothing.

We wonder how much longer those who are held prisoner will survive.

Time is running out for them. I believe it is time for our own officials to involve themselves in the effort to secure the release of all prisoners held by the Communists in Southeast Asia. I earnestly hope that in addition to signing the letter below and sending it to the Pinellas Mobile Home Association newspaper, the readers will write our own representatives and senators and to the PRESIDENT urging them to honor their obligations to these men who have suffered so much for so long.

Mrs. Gerald Gartley

Mother of Lt. Mark Gartley

P.O.W. North Vietnam

———

To His Excellency, the President

Democratic Republic of Vietnam

Many years ago, a child was born to a humble carpenter and his God-chosen wife. The child grew in wisdom and stature, and love surrounded their family. During this Christmas season, Americans are celebrating His birth through the love surrounding their families. Many, however, are separated because of the misfortunes of war and human misunderstandings. Please accept this letter as our earnest plea in behalf of "our sons in Vietnam," that they may soon be home with their families …basking in the light of that love.

In the meantime, we request that the prisoners be identified and allow regular mail between the men and their families; also, that Hanoi admit the International Council of Red Cross representatives to inspect the prisoner of war facilities and allow repatriation of the sick and wounded.

"Each man can interpret another's experience only by his own."

—Thoreau

———

Signature

———

Address"' [3]

"I wonder what response this newsletter plea will get," Min Lee said to Gerry after reading it aloud to him. "I'm so glad they put it in the paper word-for-word as I gave it to them."

"More people might take notice of it at this time of year," replied Gerry. "Christmas and all."

"You would think so, but Lord only knows what will actually touch people's hearts. So many seem to have forgotten the war."

More and more, Min Lee felt that people had decided the war was a mistake, they spoke out against it, and then promptly forgot about it. This infuriated her as men were still dying and prisoners were still held. This was a side of human nature that she struggled to understand.

The Gartley's Maine home newspaper also ran a list of 368 pilots who had been captured in North Vietnam between August 5, 1964 and November 15, 1970. The alphabetized list had been in an AP release. The list was given to Rennie Davis, a representative of Cora Weiss, co-chairman of the Committee of Liaison with Families of Detained Servicemen. The same list had been given to Senator Edward M. Kennedy of Massachusetts and Senator J. William Fulbright of Arkansas. [4]

Min Lee cut the list out of the paper and looked at it again and again. She would touch her right index finger on number 131, Gartley, Markham Ligon, Lt. JG. (7036440)—her son, a name, rank, and serial number on a piece of newsprint.

CHAPTER 13

Becoming an Activist

Min Lee and Gerry were pleased to see Mark on a special American television showing of a Canadian Broadcasting Company film the first week of January, 1971. Newsman Michael MacClear was the director, but Newsweek magazine in their January 11th issue wrote that it was clear the North Vietnamese were the directors of the film.[1] MacClear was only allowed to ask innocuous questions like their identity, their daily routine, their mail privileges, and views on the war. Newsweek reported that the questions were screened in advance and the answers were reviewed by a military censor. Only two POWs, Walter Eugene Wilber and Robert James Schweitzer, both commanders in the U.S. Navy, were allowed to talk on the camera. Mark was not. Both men talked of volley ball or basketball games, musical programs or Communist films, visiting a Cathedral in town for Christmas, and receiving mail and packages. Although neither men condemned the United States, they condemned the war and said the U.S. needed to get out of Vietnam.

The White House and the Pentagon condemned the film and called it propaganda and stated it was "violating the spirit of the Geneva Convention."[2]

The U.S. state department did not agree with the number of POWs the North Vietnamese reported in an interview of Vietnamese Premiere Pham Van Dong that accompanied the film. It also felt the film did not depict the actual treatment of the American men imprisoned.

Even though the film was controversial, it was a treat for some POW families. Gerry was quoted in the magazine article as saying. "We are just lucky to be able to see him–so many families don't even know if their sons or husbands or brothers or fathers are alive." [3] Min Lee cut the article out of the magazine and underlined Gerry's statement.

In a *Tampa Tribune* [4] article, the family of Air Force Captain Tom Browning, shot down over North Vietnam four and a half years ago was highlighted. Tom's wife Ann got to point Tom out to their four year old son Scott in the brief image of him playing basketball. Scott was born after his dad went to Vietnam. Scott's Grandfather Charlton Browning had been a prisoner of war of the Germans during WWII. Many families were feeling the frustration of having relatives imprisoned due to the war.

With the start of another new year, Min Lee thought she wasn't doing enough to get Mark home. She reminded herself that she should be working toward specific objectives and not fussing about how things shouldn't be. Instead of simply amplifying the plight of the POWs and pleading with people in the country to become more aware of their needs, she needed to be working toward an end to the war, with troop withdrawals and a return of the POWs.

Many of the League of Families of POWs' prominent members were also frustrated and beginning to think that they had to become more politically involved. League leaders like Richmond-based Phyllis Galanti, wife of pilot Paul Galanti, launched in January what she called "Bring Paul Home," which was a campaign that garnered 750,000 letters all asking for the release of the POWs and adherence to the rules of the Geneva Convention until such time. [5]

With help from business people, press, and some political groups in March, Phyllis brought these letters to Stockholm and addressed groups in both the Stockholm media and at the North Vietnamese embassy there. Disappointed in what her efforts had accomplished, she came home feeling the League's humanitarian approach wasn't working and thinking a political stand on ending the war might be necessary. While many League members were staying loyal to the Nixon government and their efforts to help the POWs, Phyllis spoke out critically about them.

In a newspaper interview with the New York Post and for the local paper in Dunedin in January, Minnie Lee was quoted as saying, "With the present administration, I see no hope of the prisoners' release or getting our troops out of Vietnam. I'm for ending this foolish war and stopping the compounding of the first mistake we made in getting in there. The government is crucifying my boy and those other boys sitting there year after year, and it's crucifying their families." [6] She went on to say, "I'm tired of the priorities the government sets. I know the prisoners come last, no matter what the government says year after year." [7]

Min Lee had kept up her correspondence with Women Strike for Peace members Ethel Taylor and Cora Weiss. It was easy as they were always sharing news with League members. She decided to accept an invitation to a conference in Toronto in three months with Cora Weiss to meet some prominent women leaders from North Vietnam even though the current U.S. administration discouraged League members from having dealings with them. The League participated in the exchange of mail with the POWs that was orchestrated by Cora Weiss and the group in which she was involved — the Committee of Liaison with Families of Servicemen Detained in North Vietnam, or COLIAFAM.

The League did so reluctantly. [8] The Vietnamese allowed very limited mail from the U.S. government, so cooperating with the people who could get mail through was necessary. Min Lee wasn't as impressed with Nixon as many of the members of the League were. She was intrigued by the influence that WSP and COLIAFAM had with the North Vietnamese. She decided going with them to this Toronto conference might be actually a step in a positive direction. She knew she would have to do some studying to prepare for this meeting and think carefully about what she would and wouldn't say.

Min Lee was also pleased to be contacted about being interviewed for a film about mothers of POWs. Churchill Films of Los Angeles, California, sent a letter to her principal at Dunedin High School on February 23rd asking permission to film a small portion of one of Minnie Lee's American

History classes, along with the interview. Her principal Mr. Freeman was delighted about the idea and enthusiastically shared the letter with Min Lee. [9]

The film company planned to send a camera crew to the high school in March. Min Lee told Gerry one evening that she thought the students would get a chuckle out of being film stars. She would have to prepare them ahead of time to be serious about the whole thing. Thank goodness the film, to be shown on Channel 13, would not air until June or July, so students would be off on summer vacation and not be able to barrage her with more questions about it than they already had after seeing it.

March 1971 would be a busy month for Minnie Lee. On top of the film crew from Los Angeles visiting the halls of Dunedin High School, she was to be one of four members of the League of Families of POWs to testify at the Subcommittee on National Security Policy and Scientific Developments of the Committee on Foreign Affairs of the House of Representatives in Washington, D.C. on March 31st. On March 22nd, a plump envelope addressed to Min arrived with very specific instructions from the committee's staff consultant John H. Sullivan. [10] Min Lee's presentation should last no longer than ten minutes and would be followed by subcommittee member questions. It also listed all the resolutions that the League members should be addressing in their testimony. Most of them were different wordings of the condemnations and protests against the North Vietnamese for not following the requirements of the Geneva Convention in their treatment of prisoners. These rules included identifying prisoners whom they hold, releasing seriously sick or injured prisoners, permitting impartial inspections of all prisoner-of-war facilities, and allowing the free exchange of mail between families and prisoners.

One resolution stood out to Min Lee as she pored over the document one evening after dinner. "Gerry, what do you think of this?" She asked.

"What?" Her husband lowered the newspaper he was reading to look over at her.

"Okay, they are talking about the fact that the prisoners have been mistreated, the North Vietnamese have refused to discuss prisoner exchange, and Nixon has announced he would withdraw one hundred and fifty thousand American troops by April of 1971. So this is the resolution:

'Resolved by the House of Representatives (the Senate concurring), That it is the sense of Congress that no further troop withdrawals should take place until an agreement has been reached by the United States with representatives of the North Vietnamese and the Vietcong regarding an exchange of all prisoners.' [11]

What does that sound like to you, Gerry?"

"Doesn't sound quite right to me. What are you thinking, Min?"

"Sounds like they're playing games with our boys' lives. Am I reading this the wrong way?"

"Don't know how else you could read it. Sounds like a game of hard ball using the POWs."

"That resolution needs to be addressed, Gerry. I need to be blunt about that being an upsetting issue."

"Be careful, Min." Gerry watched as Min Lee started silently reading the document again from the first page.

Min Lee wrote and rewrote her testimony for the hearing. She needed to have it be clear and convey exactly the right message—one that showed disapproval of the POWs being used as pawns in peace negotiations. She was more nervous about this appearance in front of the committee than she had been about getting her high school students to behave for the cameras of the L.A. film crew. Her students had turned out to be almost angels for the filming. She was proud of them. She now hoped that she would be perceived as charming to the congressional committee members as her students had been for the film crew as she gave a testimony that not all of them might receive with enthusiasm.

On March 30th, the day before the four League of Families of POWs' members were to testify, they were flown to Washington, D.C. in a military transport. Min Lee had thanked her principal for being so understanding of her time away from her classes. At the hotel on the following morning, a congressional staffer told them that Cora Weiss and some members of her peace group would also be testifying at the hearing that day. A couple League members grumbled, but Min Lee kept silent. She also kept quiet as the other three League members compared notes about the thrust of their testimony being that the only way to get the release of the POWs would be to withdraw troops from Southeast Asia. When she made her appearance in front of the committee at ten o'clock that morning, she was planning to add something else to her presentation, something a little more than just starting troop withdrawals.

Chairman Clement J. Zablocki, a representative from Wisconsin for more than twenty years, greeted Minnie Lee in Room 2172 of the Rayburn House Office Building. Min Lee had done her homework and knew Zablocki was a liberal Democrat, but he had been known for taking a strong anti-communist position and supported the Vietnam War. She also had learned that he was helping to design an early version of the War Powers Act which put presidential war-making power under congressional control, an act that Richard Nixon opposed. Min Lee smiled at this curious, Midwestern gentleman. Then she proceeded with her testimony.

"Mr. Chairman, and members of the Committee: I want to thank you for this opportunity to make my plea for meaningful action on the part of our government which will result in the return of the Prisoners-of-War.

My son, Navy Lt. Markham L. Gartley, has been a prisoner since his plane was downed over North Vietnam August 17, 1968. We did not learn of his fate until August, 1969, and we received our first letter from him in December, 1969. Since that time we have received letters written each month through January, 1971. These were delivered through the Committee of Liaison.

These, and films of prisoners released by North Vietnam, are some comfort to only a small percentage of the families of over 1600 men missing or captured.

I have come to Washington searching for the answer to the question which now haunts the families of these lonely, forsaken men. "Will I ever see my father, my husband, my son or my brother again?"

Once I had utmost faith that our government would not desert these men who so bravely carried out their military assignments-assignments which were the result of policy approved by the Congress and directed by the President.

We have been told to be brave, to continue to write, to travel, to speak, and to fight to keep their plight before the people of the world. We have been *brave, we have written, many have traveled, we have spoken, and we have campaigned long and hard to keep the public aware. But, though we <u>have</u> had more communication with some of the prisoners, we still know nothing of the fate of the hundreds who are missing in South Vietnam, Laos, and Cambodia. Our men are no nearer home than when Lt. Cdr. Alvarez was imprisoned nearly seven years ago.*

The President, his advisors, his aides, and the Secretary of Defense have assured us that the Prisoner-of-War issue has high priority in any negotiations with North Vietnam and in our over-all Southeast Asia Policy. For many of the families, the question has become, "Just <u>how</u> high on the list of priorities is the prisoner question?" And though we realize there are other problems to be considered in the over-all settlement of the Vietnam question-we wonder if these other problems have not been higher on the list than the prisoners. I am not willing to sacrifice my son for the Thieu-Ky regime if it is unable to exist with the support of the South Vietnamese people.

The North Vietnamese have said that <u>discussions</u> on the procedures of negotiations for prisoner release would be held if we set a date for total withdrawal of all United States military forces in South Vietnam.

The president feels that it is not in the national interest to set a date, and the Secretary of Defense has stated that there would be no total troop withdrawal until the prisoners are released. What no one in the administration has explained is how 50,000 troops left in South Vietnam for air and logistical support can persuade North Vietnam to negotiate seriously if 500,000 could not.

The price set for the release of the prisoners in North Vietnam, Laos, South Vietnam, and Cambodia is total withdrawal. The Vietnamization policy, with its continued American presence in South Vietnam, means that our men will die in those camps."

Min paused for a few seconds and looked up from her notes. She was surprised to see representatives looking at papers in front of them. Others appeared bored. If they had been her high school students, she would have scolded them. But they weren't, so she decided to raise her voice and continue with more emphasis on the points she wanted to get across.

"Gentlemen, I believe the majority of the American people think it is time for the United States to set a date for total withdrawal from South Vietnam. But I believe we would be wrong to set such a date without a commitment from the North Vietnamese. I believe that we should require a firm commitment from them that they will _release_ the prisoners at a date prior to that time, or on a percentage basis. As our troops are coming out, the last prisoners should come out with the last troops. Negotiations for similar commitments should be initiated with the Pathet Lao, the National Liberation Front, and with whoever represents the Cambodian Front. As you know, these hold many men who have not been accounted for. Prisoners held by the South Vietnamese should be released in a like manner.

If we withdraw any more troops _without_ such a commitment, _or_ if we set a total withdrawal date with only the _promise_ that they will enter into discussions about prisoner release, then I envision the prisoners being used as pawns in endless negotiations, demands, and counter-demands. Those boys who have languished in prison cells and tiger cages so long, and the families who have waited in vain do not deserve to be put in any such position.

It is time for the members of Congress who are evading the issue to take a firm stand one way or the other on our ultimate relations with South Vietnam. They owe it to the electorate. I urge each of you to search our own conscience and to decide what you believe.

If you decide it is in our national interest to keep a continuing force in South Vietnam in support of a government for whom we have sacrificed so much money and so many lives, you must realize that you are asking us to sacrifice more money, more lives, and the prisoners-of-war. You will be buying time with sons of mothers like me. If you believe this is in our national interest, then you should be willing to supply the necessary ingredient—which is, literally, one live body from your family.

If you refuse to take any stand for or against Vietnamization, then you are like Pontius Pilot, who stood by and then piously washed his hands. The American people will no longer accept platitudes.

If you decide that it is in our national interest to withdraw _all_ American forces from South Vietnam, then you owe it to the American people, to our boys who are laying their lives on the line every day, and to the prisoners-of-

war to make a forceful effort toward that goal immediately. Do not hesitate, do not equivocate. Do not wait until the next election, hoping that somehow the President will pull it off and get you off the hook with the American people. Three presidents have failed, and nearly 45,000 American boys have died. If their sacrifice and the billions we have spent have not given the South Vietnamese the help necessary to "hack it alone," then what leads you to believe that they will "hack it alone" if we sacrifice more boys on the battlefield, or more prisoners dying in prison?

I came to Washington to the Congress for an answer. The American people want to know. After desperate appeals to Hanoi, to Moscow, to other foreign governments, to the United Nations, and most of all to the President, where else is left for me to appeal? Or shall I try to forget that I have a son in a far-off Asian prison who is wondering year after year if his country has forsaken him and to reconcile myself to never seeing him alive?"[12]

Min Lee looked at the committee members upon finishing her statement. They were silent for a couple minutes. There were few questions for her. Then the chairman and several representatives thanked Min Lee for her testimony, and she was escorted out of the room. She decided to walk the halls and visit as many house representatives as she could before she had to return to the hotel and get ready for her trip back to Florida. She received mixed reactions from the representatives whom she was able to speak to. Some were supportive of her ideas, but some gave the impression that Vietnam was no longer a pressing issue. She found this shocking. Min Lee realized that taking such a strong stand with the committee and different representatives might land her name in the news more, but she would soon find out what a dramatic increase in requests for interviews and appearances it would actually mean.

Later, newspaper reporters questioned Min Lee not only about her statement that the POWs were being forgotten, but also about her relationship with Cora Weiss and the group COLIAFAM. Cora and she had spoken for almost an hour in D.C. Cora had testified to the senate committee that she found Mark Gartley and other POWs in healthy condition and displaying a sense of humor when she visited North Vietnam. [13] In the same article, Min Lee told reporters that this peace group had been helpful to her and had not tried to intimidate her or ask for contributions. She stated that she had even been questioned by an FBI agent about this relationship.

In another Florida newspaper from the Tampa area, Min Lee said, "At the beginning of the war, I was a hawk." [14] She went on further to explain that now both "hawks" and "doves" scare her. The hawks in government have policies that perpetuate the war with no hope for the POWs. The doves, or peace groups, rely on their faith in North Vietnam to do the right thing and return the POWs upon the withdrawal of all U.S. troops. She feels there needs to be very coordinated partial releases of POWs along with partial releases of U.S. troops as the war winds down to keep both sides from using POWs as "pawns."

Min Lee felt like she was walking a thin line in dealing with both the conservative members of the League of Families and the liberals in the peace groups. She was scared of stumbling by saying the wrong thing to the wrong person and losing track of her way to getting Mark out of North Vietnam. She always acted as a peace maker—one who tried to see both sides, but this situation was more intense than most of the things she had found herself in before now. She had little time to brood about it, though. Within a week of her D.C. testimony, she was getting ready to go with Cora Weiss to Toronto to talk with some prominent women from Southeast Asia.

CHAPTER 14

Meeting with the "Enemy"

Min Lee's stop in New York City at Cora Weiss' home before proceeding to Toronto allowed her to catch her breath and meet Cora's mother Vera Rubin. Vera was just a few years older than Min and fascinating. As a history teacher, Min Lee found Vera's work as an anthropologist interesting. She and Vera also enjoyed a smoking break together.

"Do you mind if I ask you about your accent, Min Lee?" Vera took a drag on her cigarette as she waited for her guest to reply.

"Which one?" asked Min Lee. A grin spread across her face.

"Both of them. There's more than just a Maine accent in there. Where did you live before?"

"I was born and grew up on a peach and tobacco farm in Kentucky, Vera," said Min Lee. "I'm surprised you can hear it in my speech still."

"I can hear them both."

"Vera, may I ask you about your lack of an accent, please? I understand that you and your family came from Russia," Min Lee bent forward to tap the ashes from her cigarette into an ashtray and peek around quickly to admire the beautiful patio they sat on that day.

"I was born in Moscow, but I arrived as an infant. I learned to speak and went to school here." Vera and Min Lee became so involved in a conversation about their lives that Cora hated to interrupt them to let Min know it was time for them to leave for the airport.

"Where is the conference to be held?" Vera wanted to know.

"We'll be two days at the Ontario Institute for Studies in Education in Toronto. The Quakers are gracious hosts letting us stay at their Friends Meeting House. I hope it is worth our time and effort," answered Cora.

The plane ride to Toronto was a short one, and Cora and Min Lee found themselves settled in and ready for the general meeting that would start the conference that Thursday of April 8th. They were introduced to the Indo-Chinese representatives along with various peace groups, the Women Strike for Peace from the United States, the Voice of Women from Canada, and the Women's International League for Peace and Freedom. There were approximately 350 attendees from both Canada and the United States at the meeting. Professor Vo Thi The, a professor of literature at the University of Hanoi was there as was Khampheng Boupha and Khemphet Pholsena, both of Laos. Professor The Phan Minh Hien, a teacher from South Vietnam, was also in attendance.

Min Lee listened as the Southeast Asian women spoke. Some talked critically of President Nixon and disagreed with his peace proposals. They felt that the United States had to withdraw from Vietnam before the POWs would be released. One asked about the feasibility of either side of the Vietnamese retreating. It was their country, so where would they go? Some called the U.S. pilots war criminals but insisted they were still being treated humanely. The teacher from South Vietnam urged that the people there be allowed to pick their own government free of the U.S. interference. Another talked about how the countryside is being decimated and left unproductive. Many hundred thousands of people were being affected by the chemicals used to defoliate the countryside, one reported. [1] All of the women spoke candidly, something that Minnie Lee admired. She also liked the fact that they were smaller in stature as she was. At five foot three inches tall and rather "delicate" as some described her, she often felt her size worked against her. With these women, she felt comfortable.

The next morning, Min Lee and Cora met Professor Vo Thi The and her interpreter Mr. Nguyen Tri informally at their breakfast table at the Friends Meeting House where they were staying. Min found out that the professor and the others from Southeast Asia knew of her background—being a mother of a pilot who was now a POW. Cora Weiss had told them that Min Lee was for total troop withdrawal and had so testified to a U.S. House Senate Committee on March 31st. Mr. Tri told Min Lee he would take a message to Mark if she would like to write one.

Min Lee told them as diplomatically as she could that many families and members of congress were for a set date for withdrawal, and that many more would be if they were guaranteed that the POWs would be released. Min Lee soon found out that the idea of "negotiations for release of prisoners"[2] was something the Vietnamese visitors were hung up on. They told Min Lee they would talk release when a date for U. S. troop withdrawal was set. Phrases like "we will talk release when date is set" and "depends on good faith" were stated over and over again to Min Lee. They wanted her to realize that they were honest people. Min Lee's idea of "beginning negotiations" sooner was met with "when all the troops are out."

Even though the meeting remained friendly, Min Lee could feel that repeating their sides again and again was getting them nowhere and the subject might as well be closed. Mr. Tri asked for Mark's name, and pulled out a file that had POW's names on it. He put a check by Mark's name.[3]

Min Lee then tried to start the Laos, Cambodia, and South Vietnam discussions. She pitched the idea that it would help the peace movement if they would work to release names of POWs and set up liaisons for communication as the DRV or North Vietnamese had done. She spoke slowly and repeated herself several times. Mrs. The told her that they could not speak for them.

That evening Min Lee told Cora she thought she had spoken poorly on that subject. Cora said she had talked further with them and tried to clarify Min Lee's presentation. Also, that evening at about five o'clock, Min Lee talked with the two women from Laos, Khamphing Bouplha and Khemphet Pholsena. She again made a plea for liaisons for better communications.

This time she felt she was well received. The women also did make it a point to tell Min that the U.S. pilots were war criminals acting out Nixon's policy of aggression, but that they were being treated humanely. As the press was waiting to interview the Southeast Asian women, handshakes and good wishes were exchanged. Min thought she heard one of them repeat to her that "prisoners would be released when war over." Things were rushed and communications were difficult with the different languages.[4]

Later, Min Lee discovered that the Toronto papers emphasized the differences between the groups and the strong words of Professor The more than they really had to. This disappointed her as she thought they had made some headway at the conference. Once back home in Dunedin, Min Lee felt slightly discouraged. Going to Toronto had been a long, tiring trip. She wondered when she would actually feel like a clear breakthrough was made in all of these meetings, hearings, and conferences. She was tired. She told herself she had the right to be fatigued. She was a woman in her fifties playing with a possible diagnosis of Lupus. And then there were her history lectures for school to get back to planning. But before she would take care of that, she would have a cigarette and her drink—George Dickel Tennessee whiskey with ginger ale on the rocks. Even after years of living with the Yankees in Maine, Min Lee was still a southern girl at heart. While rocking in her chair and watching the beautiful west coast Florida sunset, she held Mark's smiling face in her mind's eye for just a bit.

CHAPTER 15

Summer of Meetings and Press in Beaver Creek

Beaver Creek was a welcome respite for Min Lee after the overly active late winter and spring of 1971. She sat at the shore of Moosehead Lake with her eyes closed and enjoyed the warmth of the sun and the repetitive splashing of the waves. Of course, her cigarette was just right for this moment, too. She exhaled and grinned as she overheard Gerry scolding a camp worker for not properly cleaning out a canoe. It was good to be home. She had noticed while in Greenville to do some shopping that people seemed to take a second look at her as she passed by. She wondered whether she was just being paranoid, or if she was becoming a bit of a celebrity in this tiny Maine area. After all, a glimpse of her had been seen on the CBS news at the end of April on a report about people concerned about POWs.

Min Lee wasn't in Beaver Creek long before she received an official invitation to the premiere of a film. The film entitled *And Another Family for Peace* was to open at the Senate Auditorium in D.C. on June 15th with a reception to follow. The production was done by the peace group Another Mother for Peace, founded by Barbara Avedon, who was known for writing the Donna Reed show. In fact, Donna Reed Owen, the lead actress, was a member of the group. Several other celebrity names were involved, such as Bess Myerson, Joanne Woodward, and Betsy Palmer. Prominent politicians' wives were expected to be in attendance for the opening, including Mrs. George McGovern, the presidential candidate's wife and Mrs. Edmund Muskie, wife of the senator from Maine.

Min Lee was intrigued by all this. She had heard of this group and seen their yellow and black Mothers' Day cards with the slogan "War is not healthy for children and other living things." Inside the card read "For my Mother's Day gift this year, I don't want candy or flowers. I want an end to killing. We who have given life must be dedicated to preserving it. Please talk peace." [1] This reminded Min Lee of the Women Strike for Peace slogan that was not anti-anything but pro-peace and protection of offspring. Min Lee understood that other famous actresses like Debbie Reynolds and Lauren Bacall were members although they were not listed to be there at the opening, A few men sneaked in as members, such as Paul Newman and Robert Vaughn.

Min Lee wondered what she would wear if she actually decided to attend this affair. Plus, it was a good hike from Beaver Creek to D.C. Could she ever get Gerry in a tuxedo? Ultimately, she and Gerry had invited people over to view the documentary that Min had been involved in by Churchill Films that would be broadcast on CBS June 12th. She would have to pass up the fancy D.C. affair, but it tickled her to be invited.

Toward the end of July, Min Lee went to speak to the Moosehead Lake Women's Club in Greenville about the POW situation. She was pleased to have twenty-six club members and twelve guests in attendance. She used quotes from her testimony before the congressional committee in March to emphasize her feelings of urgency on the subject. She was well received. *The Moosehead Gazette* reported afterwards that "Mrs. Gartley's first-hand knowledge of the plight of our war prisoners makes her an ideal person to listen to. Her interesting, tragic description of the lives these men lead make it impossible to comprehend that there are still countries where life is considered worthless." [2]

Min Lee read the short article aloud to Gerry and Jim at lunch. "Maybe we are making some headway in the idea of ending the war?" Min Lee said as she put the newspaper down on the table. "Last summer, I was rather discouraged by the apathy that I felt around here."

"Takes some folk a while, Min," Gerry announced with a mouthful of sandwich. Jim nodded his head in agreement while reaching for a cookie.

As the summer wore on, news of a POW release appeared in a Swedish newspaper. Ken Buckley of the *Bangor Daily News* [3] interviewed Gerry about it. Supposedly, 183 prisoners would be released.

"There must be something to it." Gerry told Buckley. "If there wasn't some truth to it, it would never have been printed."

Buckley proceeded to report "But Gartley isn't getting overly excited about the news, which hasn't been substantiated as yet. He does however believe that there is some truth that the North Vietnamese are thinking of releasing some of their captives. 'They may let a few go to show they are honorable men of their word,' he said."

Buckley also reported that three other Mainers had been imprisoned by the North Vietnamese for many years now, including Captain Robert I. Biss of Bangor, Captain Allen R. Carpenter of Sanford, and Major Roger D. Invalson also of Sanford.

Buckley interviewed Min Lee about the news of prisoner release and found her less optimistic than her husband. She told Buckley that "President Nixon and his advisor Henry Kissinger were putting the lives of POWs far back behind the list of priorities." [4] Buckley reported her as saying "most of the families of the 1,600 missing men are now realizing what I came to know over a year ago. This is, that in spite of the pats on the back, the sympathetic words and promises that they (the government) will not forget the prisoners, is not true. The prisoners are in fact way down on the priority list. In fact recent statements by Secretary Rogers and Senator Dole reveal that they have written off the prisoners. Mr. Nixon could bring them all home if he would set a date for a withdrawal of all American forces from South Vietnam. But he will not negotiate in Paris because he has never intended to withdraw all

American forces. He hopes to placate the American public with constant references to his 'winding down of the war.' The present administration believes it is in our national interests to support the in-democratic suppressors and correct Thieu's government in South Vietnam with as much military force as is necessary – with only American planes, if possible, because casualty lists are shorter, if only airmen are lost. This is what President Nixon means by having a flexible policy while he refuses to commit himself to really ending the American involvement in South Vietnam by a set date. It couldn't be to keep Southeast Asian countries from falling to the Chinese like dominoes as we are now playing ping pong and having dinner parties with the Chinese." [5] Min did close the interview with a plea to the public to talk to their elected officials.

A couple days later, Gerry laughed as he finished reading the article and set his paper down. "You're not one to mince words, are you, my dear?"

"What's the sense of that, Gerry? The time has come for straight talk." She gave Gerry what he called her "teacher glare." He said no more.

CHAPTER 16

‮ و‬

A Schism in the League of Families of POWs & MIAs

In the middle of August, Min Lee packed up early for herself and Jim and left camp for Florida. She had a meeting to attend with some of the League members and their families. Candidates had been declared to run for president for both political parties' primaries. She had offered to go to a meeting with candidate George Wallace, the governor of Alabama, who was running as a Democrat instead of an Independent. It was his second attempt for the White House. Wallace had shown a concern for the POWs and MIAs and had visited the families of several of these military men. George posed for a picture with League members and their families at the meeting. Min Lee was disappointed when his campaign speeches after the meeting never mentioned POWs or their precarious plight. [1]

School opened without any problems that fall of 1971. Min Lee was getting ready for the national meeting of the League of Families of POWs/MIAs in Washington, D.C. Min Lee, and several other members now felt it was time to become more political and take a stand about ending the war. There was a definite schism in the group. Some members were ready to

become more politically vocal than they had been before while others were
for going along with the edicts of the Nixon administration. They felt it
necessary to remain patient and quiet about their feelings concerning the war
itself.

Min Lee told some League members, "Advisors from the Pentagon said
we could not even advocate legislation without losing our tax-exempt status."[2]
She and others still pushed for the passing of a resolution that would allow
League members to become more politically active instead of staying simply a
humanitarian organization.

About 500 members, including Min Lee, formed a splinter group,
or an internal political action committee, called POW-MIA Families for
Immediate Release. Min Lee gave the following speech at the convention
with the hopes of swaying the vote for allowing political stands and action in
the League:

*"Each of us here today has an obligation to our loved ones who cannot
speak for themselves and whose situation is becoming more desperate each day.
It is our obligation to forget pride, dignity, petty differences, and prejudice. We
must speak out, we must write, we must lobby, we must even beg, we must do
whatever we believe will secure their release – and we must never relax our
efforts.*

*I said 'secure their release' because surely we hold hopes that each of the
missing is a prisoner. And so, when we speak of prisoners, we speak of those of
whom, (after all these years), our government can tell us nothing. We cannot
accept Senator Dole's writing off of the missing when he said that the prisoners
represent less than one-half of one percent of all the Americans who have died in
South Vietnam.*

*It is no wonder that we who listen closely to statements by high officials
are frantic with fear that all our men have been written off as expendable. The
POW – MIA problem has been shoved on the back burner, swept under the rug,
in the hopes that it will be forgotten as the public is duped into believing the war
is practically over.*

I ask you, please, to consider the following:

1.Our men were fighting a war, and wars are fought for political purposes.

2. *Wars are over when one side has totally defeated the other, or when each side agrees at negotiations to accept what political gains they can get.*
3. *Our actions will not make our men political tools. By the nature of this war they are. They will be used by the other side to obtain political gains. Right now – their price is a withdrawal date. What will it be in the fall of '72 when we are down to that relatively small residual force?*
4. *Prisoners are released when wars are over.*
5. *MIAs are accounted for after fighting has stopped.*

It is our obligation to use every means to inform the American people of these facts and to urge them to express themselves to their elected officials as diligently as we urged them to write to Hanoi. I believe that if we do not exert the last ounces of our energy toward achieving release and final accounting within this coming year, we can justifiably be held responsible if our men stay in prison indefinitely. Each of you knows the apathy of your friends and acquaintances, and the little concern for them now shown by the press, by television, and even by most elected officials. The American people have forgotten them! – especially since Mr. Perot told the nation on the CBS Documentary that the prisoners were being treated so much better and that their morale was higher than last year.

When I say OUR obligation, I mean each of us – individually. How many letters have you written? – One a day? How many arms have you twisted to get others to write to their Congressmen or to the President?

But how much more effective we would be if we could act collectively, if we could be a powerful lobby for our men – not only in the halls of Congress and in the White House, but in the newspaper offices, TV stations, and wherever we could make our voices heard."

Min Lee paused. She now worried that what she had written next was too personal and emotional. She looked at her audience. They seemed bored with the political talk she had been giving. Maybe this sensitive part of her speech would reach more of them. She closed her eyes for a minute and then proceeded.

"I have not shed a tear since my son was shot down – I, too, am determined to win or to go down fighting – but I can cry when I think of what we could do

and of what we <u>have not</u> done. We could have had many times this number of families and friends here to fight with us. We <u>could</u> have been such a powerful force that the government could not have ignored us. We <u>could</u> have acted always with the good of our country and our men as our goal, rather that timidly accepting the advice and guidance of those whose jobs depend upon whoever is setting our foreign policy – whether it is the President or a Mr. Kissinger.

For those of you who thought that 'Political Action' meant backing a candidate, I assure you nothing could be more wrong – even impossible. It means taking the action I have described – informing the people, <u>keeping</u> them informed, and asking them to back the only policy which will bring our prisoners home and bring an accounting of those still missing.

No need to cry over what 'might have been.' We are all to blame. <u>This</u> is the critical year for our men.

If we do not vote to become such a collective force because (even though we have a common goal) we bicker and disagree, then let us – as a League of Families – all join in actions on which there is no controversy. I was appalled to have one of the members in the Washington office of the League tell me recently that 'no action was going on because no one could think of anything to do!!' There are numbers of bills lost in Congressional Committees that our League could inform us of. <u>Surely</u>, this is not illegal under our charter!! There are <u>many</u> things Sec. Laird's 'high-level' task force on the POWs and MIAs could do to help our men that they are not doing. The League could initiate such action. There is information of interest to us all that can be better disseminated than in the past.

And those members of the League who, like me, feel this sense of urgency that this is the year – that this is the critical time of the year – and that we must not waste a day – can meet here together for a few minutes after this meeting is adjourned to take the first step toward raising a groundswell of public pressure to bring this war to an honorable end – not a dribbling out of the lives of the wives who now live in limbo – not knowing, and of the lives of our loved ones who are living in the hell of despair and abandonment.

Last Sunday I listened to an Air Force Captain speak on the POW – MIA problem. He said that only a miracle could bring the boys home and urged his audience to pray for such a miracle.

I do not underestimate the power of prayer – but the Walls of Jericho did not fall until the Israelites had marched around them <u>seven</u> times, and blown their trumpets. We must do the same!!!" [3]

After giving the speech, Min Lee led several League members out to the gates of the White House and picketed with signs reading, "Withdrawal Date Now for POWs – MIAs" and "Bring Them Home." [4] Some of the picketers wore buttons on their apparel reading "P.O.W. – M.I.A.s Number One, Not THIEU." [5] These buttons were to express concern with Nixon's South Vietnamization policy that many felt would leave the POWs and MIAs forgotten in the process. The women had not changed out of their clothes they had worn for the convention, so they were in nice dresses and pumps. Min Lee complained to friends, "We blistered our feet." [6]

A few press photographers snapped pictures of their efforts at the picket line, but the women did not know if they had caused much of a stir until the convention reconvened at the Statler Hilton, and a surprise guest appeared to talk to the League. President Nixon was there. Some League members heard that he had come because of the upcoming election year. Others said that Henry Kissinger had found out that a political action committee had formed within the League's ranks, and he was informed "about the possibility of a revolt against the Administration by our Organization." [7] Nixon, with Defense Secretary Melvin Laird and General William Westmoreland standing behind him, spoke to the League about the POWs and MIAs being a priority and how many avenues were being pursued to get them out, many that could not be disclosed. In closing remarks, he said, "I am just so proud of how great you have been and I am not going to let you down." [8] He also warned, "We are dealing with a savage enemy, one with no concern for humanitarian ideals." [9]

Nixon's appearance worked, but not the way Min Lee wanted. The following day, a majority of League members voted to not take any political stands even though Senator Ted Kennedy had told them in his appearance before Nixon's visit that "POWs were 'rotting' in Communist prisons because the Nixon administration had not responded to the July 1st proposal of the Vietcong in Paris," [10] and many League members had shared that several senators had refused to speak with them about the war, some going as far as sending aides out from their offices to get rid of League members. [11] The League also passed resolutions to make any members taking a political stand to do so as an individual and not in representation of the League. They also voted to send a delegation to the United Nations to promote concern for the plight of the POWs and MIAs. They did decide to reconvene in the spring and not wait a whole year, so they could possibly use some of their clout in the elections happening in the fall of 1972.

None the less, the PAC formed within the League had an effect on the organization. One of the League's former leaders and organizers, Sybil Stockdale, whose high-ranking Navy officer husband Jim had been a POW since 1965, commented, "It didn't do any harm at all to have a radical fringe group as part of our organization." [12] When quizzed about the women who had picketed in front of the White House, Sybil said, "It didn't hurt to let the White House know our loyalty was wearing thin." [13]

Not every League member was placated by President Nixon's words. Some like Mrs. William Mullen, whose husband, a Marine pilot, was shot down in 1966, was quoted as saying, "We've been told for so long not to say anything because it would aid Hanoi. Well, being quiet and leaving everything up to the President has not done anything. The President is turning the fate of our men over to President Thieu. So I, for one, am going to start speaking out." [14] She wouldn't be the only one to have this opinion. Although the League had chosen not to officially become political, many members decided to overwhelm the administration and congress with letters pleading for concern about their POWs and MIAs. Feelings of frustration were at a high level as the convention ended.

The October 11th issue of *Time* featured pictures of Min Lee and other ladies picketing in front of the White House. It had an article about the dissent in the League and how some were beginning to speak out. Min Lee cut the article out to show Gerry and friends and wrote in the margin of it, "After I organized a White House picket which caused some notice around Washington, Mansfield's office was in favor of it." [15] Supporting the end of the war to get the POWs out. Mansfield had been recently supporting Nixon's policy of South Vietnamization but decided that the release of the

POWs should take priority over helping set up President Thieu. Senate Majority Leader Mike Mansfield also had been involved in amendments, such as the McGovern-Hatfield Amendment that would place restrictions on the president's power to wage war, and resolutions to try to encourage President Nixon to bring an end to the war. Min Lee found it comforting to know that many members of Congress were criticizing Nixon's continuation of the war.

A month after returning to Dunedin from the League convention, Min Lee received news of Bob Hope, a popular comedian and celebrity involved in entertaining U.S. military troops since World War II, visiting Tampa to talk to an audience at the Bayfront Arena in October about the plight of the POWs/MIAs. She and Mary Doak, both mothers of a POW, met with Mr. Hope at the Tampa Airport to share their knowledge and feelings on the subject. Min Lee and Mary were admirers of Hope and his work for the POWs and were thrilled to have a picture taken of them flanking the celebrity for the newspapers. Hope told them he was asked about the POW/MIA situation everywhere he went. [16] Meeting with this celebrity who supported the effort to bring them home was a bright spot for Min Lee in the otherwise arduous fight to demand attention for her Mark, and the sons, husbands, and fathers biding time in prison camps in Southeast Asia.

CHAPTER 17

New York and Dr. Spock

Cora Weiss asked Min Lee to come to New York City the following month of November 1971 and speak at a peace rally that would take place in Central Park. It was expected to be a large gathering, and Min Lee was fascinated to find out that Dr. Benjamin Spock, the famous baby doctor, would also be speaking to the audience. Min Lee immediately started working on her speech even though she worried about leaving her son Jim alone again so soon after the convention in D.C. Jim struggled on his own, and Gerry would not be in Florida with them until the end of the month. Somehow it did not seem fair to Min Lee when she stopped to think that both of her sons were in trouble and in need of her concern — one a prisoner of war in a foreign land and the other a prisoner of sorts of a mental illness that kept him from achieving what he should be able to do with his high intelligence.

Min Lee decided to prepare Jim to handle things for a couple days as best she could, and she flew up to New York Friday night for the rally on Sunday, with a return ticket in her purse to fly right back to Dunedin on Sunday night. Min Lee was invited to stay at the Fifth Avenue penthouse of Cora's mother Dr. Vera Rubin. When she looked up where it was after being given Vera's address, she was excited to discover that the penthouse overlooked the highly touted Guggenheim Museum. She was quite taken by Vera's place when she arrived in Manhattan. The high rise building at 1080 Fifth Avenue was in a beautiful area on the east side of Central Park. Min Lee stood for a few minutes after Vera invited her in and looked at the view.

"I never knew such a beautiful area in New York City existed," Min Lee said as she stood at the large picture windows. "The park is really lovely."

"I do have a lovely view of the reservoir," said Vera with a grin.

"I love a view of the water. It's not as big as Moosehead Lake where our camp is in Maine, but it's nice, Vera."

Min Lee kept a serious mind about the peace event she would take part in. Senator Vance Hartke, an Indiana Democrat, and Congresswomen Bella Abzug, a Democrat representing a district in New York and a well-known, outspoken feminist, would speak as well. The event would be considered the final piece of the fall offensive against the war in Vietnam, a campaign that had started with Moratorium Day rallies across the country. In Washington on the Ellipse, approximately 3,000 people gathered while in Boston on the Commons, 4,000 gathered, but New York City would have the largest group. There at the Sheep Meadow, an estimated total of 20,000 people gathered.

Senator Hartke told a reporter, "This war has seared our souls, dulled our minds, and come perilously close to destroying us as a country, and that it may yet do." [1] Dr. Spock asked people in the crowd to send letters and telegrams demanding an end to the war to President Nixon. Spock was quoted as saying that action needed to be taken to get rid of "that smirky, slick, oily smile of Nixon, who thinks he has conned us." [2]

Min Lee watched the whole event from behind the podium as she had been issued a backstage pass. The affair had started with a parade of thousands of men, women, and children from the city marching up the Avenues of the Americas to the Sheep Meadows in Central Park. They were protesting a wage freeze, racism, goings on in Attica Prison, but most of all the Vietnam War with chants of "Out Now." Forty men carried a fifty-foot banner that read "Stop the Bombing-U.S. Out of Indochina Now." [3]

The crowd was a mix of students, elderly, union delegates, and community organizers, among others. People from New Jersey, Nassau and Suffolk Counties, and Connecticut joined them, too. In some spots, protestors marched thirty abreast as they chanted peace slogans and waved signs. The protestors were dressed in everything from Army fatigues, blue jeans, slack suits, to business suits. Pamphlets and underground newspapers were passed out, and vendors sold buttons and pennants demanding the resolution of all kinds of social ills. They were met with little resistance. At one point some construction workers jeered them, but no one responded. Fifty or so demonstrators stood just outside a fence set up near the speaker platform and threw stones and insults at Senator Hartke, but he was not hurt. It was a peaceful day of strolling, chatting, and eating ice cream and pretzels. [4]

As Min Lee looked out over the large throng of people, she was glad she was where she was behind the podium. When she was introduced, she tried to show no signs of nervousness as she adjusted the microphone down from where a taller speaker had set it. She took a deep breath and began:

"My son has been a prisoner in North Vietnam since August 1968. Once I had utmost faith that our government would not desert their men who so bravely carried out their military assignments – assignments which were the result of policy approved by Congress and directed by the President. But it is no wonder that we who listen closely to statements by administrative officials are frantic with fear that all our men have been written off as expendable. The POW-MIA problem has been shoved on the back burner, swept under the rug, in the hopes that it will be forgotten as the public is duped into believing the war is practically over.

I feel a great urgency that this is the year, that this is the critical time of the year for our men held in prison – and for America. For I am afraid that unless we somehow make total disengagement from South Vietnam a reality this year – or failing this – we make it a major issue in the next election, then those who say that it is in our national interest to maintain residual United States military forces in Vietnam will manage to set a pattern for foreign policy which could last as long as the China policy which they are now admitting was wrong!

I do not believe the American people want the bombing, the killing, the maiming, and the drain of our resources to continue indefinitely.

I do not believe the American people really want a foreign policy which will condemn the prisoners of war to rot in those prisons.

I want to believe that Americans care – and my faith in their sincerity lies greatly on the hundreds of thousands of letters they were persuaded to write to Hanoi. I maintain that if they had directed their letters to Washington instead of to Hanoi then the war would really have been over, and mothers like me would have their sons at home.

We were told that Hanoi is responsive to American public opinion. If this is true, then our own elected officials should be infinitely more responsive. Why aren't they?? One reason is apathy – I talk constantly with people who seem to listen, who agree, who are sympathetic, **but** *who turn the conversation to last night's TV, or the latest ballgame when I mention writing letters to Washington.*

We who are really concerned about our country – in war and peace – must somehow redouble our efforts to change this apathy to action. We must arouse this apathy to action for the Mansfield Amendment.

But the cruel truth is that Mr. Nixon's 'Plan for getting us out of the war' never meant total withdrawal. Total withdrawal is the price set by the North Vietnamese and the NCF for the release of the prisoners. The administration says 'Though the prisoners are important, we cannot lose sight of our national objective.'

When I asked a White House spokesman 'What is the national objective for which the prisoners are being sacrificed?' He replied, 'It is the right of the South Vietnamese for self-determination.' He said we must support their government with military forces as long as necessary.

I am not willing to sacrifice my son for the Thieu government if, after all, sacrifice cannot exist without the support of its own people. The administration says 'We cannot trust the other side when they offered release of POWs in exchange for a set date.' I say, 'We haven't tried.' We have never said to them 'Will you release the prisoners of war if we set a date for withdrawal?' We have only accused them of not meaning what they say.

We have never seriously negotiated in Paris – because such negotiations would involve our military withdrawal. The administration says to the families of the POWs 'The prisoner issue is a humanitarian issue.' The most

humanitarian thing they can do is to bring them home. We will treat them well.
   1 But wars are fought for political gain.
   2 Prisoners are released when wars are over.
   3 Let's negotiate at Paris. Let's set a date.
   And mothers' sons from both sides can return home." [5]

Min Lee had changed the last line of her speech from "American mothers' sons" to "mothers' sons from both sides," and she was glad she did. She wanted to show empathy for both sides of this unjust conflict. The ending of her presentation was well received. She stood for a minute and looked out over the diverse crowd. She wondered how President Nixon could ignore the protests of so many of his fellow countrymen. When she turned, she saw her fellow speakers smiling at her. She smiled back modestly and bowed her head, but she knew she had done well. There wouldn't be much time to bask in any glory, though, as she was whisked back to Dr. Rubin's penthouse to gather her belongings and scoot to the airport. She hoped she could catch a nap on the plane.

Shortly after Min Lee arrived back in Dunedin, she unpacked a letter that she had received at the rally and had glanced over quickly before she gave her speech. It was from the student government of Manhattan College, Bronx, New York. Now she had the time to read it thoroughly. The letter commended Min for speaking at the peace rally. The students spoke of her courage and dedication to peace in Southeast Asia. A line that particularly touched her heart read, "Few have as much right and moral authority to demand peace as you, the mother of a flyer imprisoned in North Vietnam." [6] The students told Min Lee they knew they were speaking for millions across the country. The letter was signed by the student body president as well as twelve other student leaders, including fraternity leaders, sport team captains, the editor of their school newspaper, a leader of a Vietnam veterans group, and the leader of a group for student Black unity.

Min Lee penned a response immediately. In her letter, she wrote, "Dear Young Men, I was deeply moved by your letter thanking me for speaking for peace and the Mansfield Amendment at the November 6th Rally in Central Park. It gave me a warm feeling on that cold afternoon in New York to know that young men, not far removed from the age of my son, cared enough to make such a gesture. And I shall cherish your letter and save it to show to him if he ever returns home. He, and all those held prisoner in Southeast Asia, have been deserted by their government. One cause for my concern about his rehabilitation if he does return is that he may be embittered. I shall add your letter to the small stock of evidence I am accumulating to show him that there were people who cared. I do not believe I need commendation for any speeches or actions I make for peace, for I feel so strongly that this is the duty of all who know the truth. We must somehow arouse the people to demand that our government take action for peace." [7] She closed by thanking them for their thoughtfulness and caring. Min once again was glad she had made the effort to attend the rally. It raised her spirits.

Gerry arrived in Dunedin for Thanksgiving and with him came his usual news of Maine. This had a soothing effect on Min Lee, even though he complained about the Florida telephone ringing constantly for Min Lee with requests for interviews and appearances. A call about an interview from Dan Rather of CBS impressed Gerry. He teased her about being a celebrity.

The three Gartleys shared ideas about a Christmas box that would be sent to Mark. On the kitchen table, Min Lee had the usual items she had collected. A Beaver Creek Store tee shirt to remind him of home, long underwear for warmth as they heard that winter nights could get cold in North Vietnam, a fluffy towel, instant coffee, and a picture of a woman obviously taken in Greenville just this last summer.

"What is this picture all about, Min?" Gerry held the picture to examine it more closely.

"Mark asked for 'a picture of my beautiful old playmate' [8] in a letter we received last summer. This is a girl he dated in high school," Min Lee explained as she folded the long underwear as flat as possible.

Jim put his coke down on the table and asked, "Why in the world would he want a picture of her, Mom? She's married and has a bunch of kids."

"I have no idea, but that's the only thing I could think of. What do you think he meant?" his mother replied.

Jim and his father slyly exchanged quick, comical glances and continued to supervise Min's packing in silence.

The Gartleys had a quiet Christmas the next month. They sent out the League Christmas cards in hopes that they would keep the POWs in people's thoughts. Min Lee also sent an editorial to a local paper containing an excerpt of a poem written by Barbara Mullen of California whose husband had been a POW for five years. It read:

"Christmas is sad and lonely and tears, when he's been gone for so many years.

A holiday gift is death to some delivered by us in the shape of a bomb.

Our President had a peace plan, he said. Why then are so many more dead?

Weary people shrug and pretend,

It's all true and the war is at end.

Talk of brotherhood and kindness and cheer, tell all your friends

It's been a good year.

Peace on earth is a lie, and death is sadness.

They'll never make it back, for mankind is madness." [9]

To accompany the poem, Min Lee wrote, "As a mother of a Navy lieutenant who is being held in a North Vietnam prison, Mrs. Mullen's words hit home." [10] She figured a few harsh words in poetic form might reach some people who hadn't listened yet. She didn't care if she was being a Scrooge.

CHAPTER 18

Nixon's Lady from Florida

After a pleasant Christmas, the new year of 1972 started with a bang. Min Lee found out that Sybil Stockdale, wife of Captain James Stockdale who was the highest ranking Navy officer held as a prisoner since 1965, had recently given a biting comment to a reporter doing an article about the discouragement felt by the League members. Mrs. Stockdale was quoted as saying, "Kissinger tells us the administration is doing all that can be done, but we tend to believe that less and less. If there's no progress by May, I think we should make the POWs a major issue in the presidential campaign- -even if it means becoming militantly anti-administration and supporting a Democrat."[1] Min Lee gathered copies of this article to share while commenting about how it was high time.

On January 2, Dan Rather spoke with President Nixon on a live broadcast. The Gartleys were tuned in. Min waited anxiously to see if Dan Rather would make any reference to his recent interview with her. She didn't think he would. He did. The conversation, broadcast on CBS television and their radio station on Sunday night at 9:30pm EST, started right away with Dan Rather questioning the president about his campaign themes of "A generation of peace" and "Prosperity without war." [2] Nixon talked about the country after the end of the war. Dan Rather then proceeded to question President Nixon on his resumption of widespread bombing of North Vietnam and asked him to explain the military benefits of such a campaign. Nixon said he had no choice as the North Vietnamese had violated the conditions of the bombing halt. He also talked about a reduction in American deaths and a continuation of troop withdrawal on our part.

Dan Rather then switched gears and asked the president about a recent statement he had made for TIME magazine, in which he had said, "The issue of Vietnam will not be an issue in the campaign as far as this Administration is concerned, because we will have brought the American involvement to an end." [3] President Nixon talked about whether or not the peace talks in Paris would work or if the U.S. would have to maintain some residual troops in Vietnam and have more U.S. air strikes on the North Vietnamese.

"How can you campaign saying you have ended the American involvement?" asked Rather. [4] The president again reiterated all he had done to draw the war down as far as casualties and increasing troop withdrawals, but he also talked about what a mess he had inherited from past administrations.

Min Lee was fussing to Gerry and Jim about the conversation simply being the same old tired excuses when Gerry hushed her as he heard Rather say something about a lady from Florida. That was when they heard, "Mrs. Gerald Gartley, from Florida, who is the mother of a twenty-seven year old Navy Lieutenant who is a prisoner. (sic) Her question, which I take this opportunity to ask on her behalf is, have we ever asked the North Vietnamese and the Provisional Revolutionary Government if they will release the POWs and guarantee the safety of our withdrawing troops if we set a date for the withdrawal of all U.S. forces from South Vietnam." [5]

Min Lee froze in her seat. She made fists with her hands on her knees as she listened to the president's reply. "That was floated out this fall, the North Vietnamese totally rejected it," Nixon replied to Rather. [6]

"That was publicly done?" asked Mr. Rather.

"That was publicly done, that is correct," replied President Nixon. [7]

"I don't believe he said that on public television!" hissed Min Lee. "This is a lie." Gerry sat and shook his head. Jim was upset to see his mother so angry.

The president continued to talk about the times he felt this proposal had been made to the North Vietnamese, along with reminding Mr. Rather and the viewers that many negotiations were done in private. The public ones in Paris were just a few of many discussions.

President Nixon then said, "In due time and at the appropriate time, our lady from Florida and the others will realize that we have gone the extra mile as far as the POWs are concerned. I do not want to disclose any further details because negotiations are under way." [8]

Min Lee immediately sent a note to Californian Congressman Robert L. Leggett, whom she knew was for a complete troop withdrawal. Within four or five days, Min Lee received word from Leggett's legislative counsel Robert M. Sherman about the congressman sending a letter to the president asking for clarification of his response to her question. Sherman agreed with Min Lee that the president had lied. Reporters called her for interviews.

On January 5, James D. Hughes, Brigadier General of the United States Air Force and Military Assistant to the President, sent out letters to "family members" of POWs offering "verbatim text of the conversation" between the president and Dan Rather. He stated in this letter, "In my opinion, they [the president's answers] quite clearly express the President's policy and his sincere intentions not to abandon these brave men [POWs]." [9] Min Lee wrote as a note on top of the interview transcript, "This speech [of Nixon's] caused the biggest stir about the war--and the prisoners up to this time. There had been nothing for months about the POWs. Because of my question the press besieged me. I never expected Dan Rather to mention my name. No one expected Nixon to lie." [10]

Min Lee grinned as she held the brigadier general's letter in her hands. "Guess we really hit a chord there?" she said to Gerry.

"Good God, Min!" Gerry rolled his eyes.

"Well, it is just so ridiculous of Hughes to send us all a letter like that. Did he think he was going to intimidate us into being quiet and not asking questions? The big brigadier general! Remember our neighbor back home,

Brigadier General Harrison Thyng from New Hampshire? Highly decorated fighter pilot of WW II and Korea. Came home from a brief stint in Vietnam in 1966 and resigned from the Air Force so he could talk publicly about our involvement there not being a wise idea. He was brave enough to talk against it while most people seemed to think it was a just cause."

"Probably cost him the senatorial election he ran in."

"We should have listened to him."

CHAPTER 19

Media Splash!

Later in January 1972, Min Lee joined approximately two dozen other members of the League of Families at the White House to hear and question Henry Kissinger about President Nixon's latest peace proposal. Min Lee left the meeting still a critic. The confusion over the idea that offers had been made to the North Vietnamese for troop withdrawals in exchange for prisoner release was not cleared. In a telephone interview she said, "Each side is seeking a 'victory,'" and Nixon is determined to avoid any settlement before the November election that could expose him to an attack from the right. He must be able to justify the 20,000 men who have died in Vietnam since he began his 'plan to end the war.'"[1]

Reporter Daniel Rappaport of United Press International, while covering the House of Representatives, reported the upset among League members saying, "The controversy erupted at a House foreign affairs subcommittee hearing where Deputy Assistant Secretary of State William H. Sullivan offered little hope that many of the approximately 1,200 missing in Indochina were alive. The comment evoked an emotional response from three League members who were sitting in the audience. They contended that whether true or not the United States should not be making such a statement because it would lose leverage in bargaining with the Communists for more information on the missing." [2] The League's national coordinator Mrs. Evelyn Grubb, of Virginia, was quoted as saying, "Shocking." [3] The assistant national coordinator Mrs. Donald Shay of Maryland declared, "He's just written off my son." [4]

Rappaport also interviewed Min Lee via telephone. She gave him a bleak outlook. She summarized her perspective on the situation by saying that Nixon wanted to keep the Thieu government in power and the North Vietnamese want him out and to take control of the South. The North also wants an end to the war. Nixon wants to maintain a presence to aid Thieu. The North will not release our POWs until we are out of Vietnam. Rappaport quoted her as saying, "Prisoners sit there in lonely prisons year after year. I see no more hope than in the beginning. Until there are real negotiations- -which end in compromises from each side- -there is a real danger they will rot and die there." [5]

As a result of the uproar caused by the Rather interview and the ensuing articles in the news, President Nixon decided to do a nation-wide television and radio address about striving for peace in Vietnam on January 25th. In his speech, Nixon reiterated the many things he had done to bring an end to the war. The U.S. News and World Report on February 7th summarized the president's talk as "Thirty months of secret talks were laid bare, coupled with public notice to Hanoi-and to critics at home: There will be no surrender in Vietnam." [6]

"Min, I don't understand all this, for Christ's sake," fussed Gerry as he sat sprawled on the sofa of their mobile home in Dunedin. "One side said they did; the other side said they didn't. Where's the truth actually lie if there is such a thing?"

"Well, from what I can gather, Gerry, Nixon spoke to Foreign Minister Andrei Gromyko about the POW situation, and Kissinger spoke with the Chinese Premier Chou En-lai about them, too. They claim both of these men told them that the North Vietnamese would not accept any peace negotiations yet. I believe that is what they are referring to when they talk about offers turned down," Min Lee said. "I really don't trust either of them as far as I could throw them. I've never felt so discouraged."

"Min, you can only do so much. Politics is a nasty business." The couple sat without talking. It had been a long two and a half years.

CHAPTER 20

Keep the Noise Going

The media backlash caused by Nixon's interview and subsequent speeches proved something important to Min Lee. If the subcommittee of the League that was working to end the war and bring troops home wanted to get anywhere, they had to keep hollering enough to stay in the news. Americans were forgetting about the Vietnam War. Many foolishly thought it had already ended. On January 20th, eight League members decided to work with the Fellowship of Reconciliation and the Committee of Liaison with Families of Servicemen detained in Vietnam as they organized a vigil outside the Capitol while Nixon gave his State of the Union address. The clergy joining this group were an impressive all faith collection of religious leaders, representing Protestant, Catholic, and Jewish religions.

About 400 clergymen and families of POWs and MIAs marched down East Capitol Street form the Lutheran Church of the Reformation to the Capitol grounds. Police, who told them they caused security problems, stopped the group at First Street and East Capitol, but they climbed over a wall and advanced to the edge of the Capitol parking lot and stopped at a barrier. The protestors decided to wait until President Nixon left the Capitol before advancing to the Capitol steps to hold their peaceful demonstration.[1] Before getting to the steps, they stood in the cold and occasional light showers with their protest signs and sang "We Shall Overcome." Some protest signs asked for an end to the war. Some asked people to vote Nixon out of office. Many protestors held up battery-operated, transistor radios that were broadcasting Nixon's address. When they were allowed on the steps of the east front of the Capitol, they were joined by a half dozen congressmen. The vigil lasted about twenty minutes.

Min Lee was heartened by the earnest statements made by the protestors. When her turn came to speak, she reiterated the question Dan Rather had asked President Nixon in the nationally televised interview of January 2nd about offering North Vietnam a set date for complete withdrawal of U.S. troops in exchange for the release of prisoners of war. Min Lee told the group, "President Nixon didn't tell the truth when he answered my question. Why won't the administration make this offer?"[2] Her comments were applauded by the large gathering. Min Lee closed her eyes for a moment and enjoyed the warmth of the support of these activists.

League member Valerie Kushner from Danville, Virginia, told the group, "This is the fifth State of the Union and second Presidential election year that my husband has been a prisoner of war. If I thought we were asking a lot, I might understand why it has taken so long, but it seems so easy. We're not asking that anyone risk their lives—we're asking that the killing be stopped. We're not asking families to send their husbands and sons far away to bring ours home. We're asking for all our men to be brought home."[3]

Reverend William Sloane Coffin, Yale University Chaplain, stated, "The POWs and MIAs are being used by the President as an excuse for continuing to support the Thieu regime in Saigon. It should be intolerable to all of us that our government continues the destruction of Indochina and makes these families suffer to keep a regime in Saigon that makes a mockery of the freedoms for which Americans are urged to go and risk their lives."[4]

Bishop James Armstrong spoke to the large group at the vigil about a letter that he and Sister Mary Luke Tobin were writing to all the families of POWs. This letter would explain why they were asking these families to demand that the President set a date for complete withdrawal to end the killing and gain release of the POWs and an accounting of the missing.[5] POW wife Valerie Kushner spoke up again and echoed the extreme frustration she and other families of POWs were feeling when she stated, "If the President wants to bring our nation together, he better stop this war right now. We're running out of patience."[6]

When Min Lee arrived back home to Dunedin, the feelings of support she had experienced in D.C. and dreams of bringing Mark home soon melted into pessimism and hopelessness. She pored over news articles about the peace vigil and despaired over the wide range of reporters' perspectives of it in their writing. One mistake-filled article called her "a nobody" before the Nixon interview with Dan Rather. She underlined errors in the article and wrote a big "Ha Ha" on her copy of it.[7] Her mother always said you might as well laugh as cry, but she didn't feel like laughing after reading that ridiculous account of something she considered so important. She just felt angry. She tried to tell herself she was overtired, but the negative feelings hung on her like a fog. She needed to plan for her classes next week, but she couldn't seem to motivate herself. She took refuge in her rocking chair on the front patio. That's where Gerry found her lighting a cigarette. He sat down in the chair next to her and gave her a long look.

"What?" asked Min Lee while exhaling a long puff of cigarette smoke.

"You're gonna wear yourself out, Min," Gerry replied.

"What would you like me to do? Sit around and wait?"

"Something's gotta happen soon, Min. Don't you think?"

Min Lee sat quietly and rocked and puffed. She had no answer for her husband. It was too much.

CHAPTER 21

A POW's Day

At the very end of January, the 31st, the New York Times printed a very subtle, but strong letter to the editor by James Reston, a journalist whom Min Lee had always admired. He mentioned Mrs. Gerald Gartley by name in talking about how the families of the POWs had "cut to the heart of this issue" [1] of the war and the release of the prisoners North Vietnam was holding. He said even though Democratic presidential candidates, such as Muskie, McGovern, Humphrey, and Lindsay were stumbling on over Nixon's peace terms and finding themselves "caught in a tangle of complex and ambiguous qualifications, and even in danger of seeming to be sympathetic to the enemy," [2] these families seemed to see through the quagmire and understand what Nixon's position actually was. He felt Nixon had fooled many and was gaining ground in the campaign, but Reston ended his editorial with these words:

"During the long and sharp debate that lies ahead, the President, if he sticks to his present peace terms and war aims, will be asking the American people to continue fighting, not only for the release of the American prisoners of war-but for the maintenance of his ally in Saigon, for the neutralization of all of Indochina, and for democracy in a country where the word has little meaning.

Here in Florida his complicated peace terms will be a good political issue at least until the primary voting on March 14th, but thereafter, when his military and political terms are finally analyzed and widely understood, they may well be seen not as a means to peace, but as a cause for continuing the war. And by November, that might not be a very popular argument for re-election." [3]

"What do you think of Reston's editorial, Gerry?" asked Min Lee when she saw her husband look up from reading it. They were finishing coffee at their breakfast table.

"It's great, Min, but it is not straight forward enough. He's written it in a roundabout way, don't you think?"

"I think I should write an editorial reply clarifying it. Do you think the Times would print it?"

"Worth a try, Min," said Gerry. "I think they would print it after he mentioned you by name."

Min Lee was pleased when The Times did publish her editorial entitled "A POW's Day: 'The Sun Rises, The Sun Sets." It read:

"In a recent editorial The Times said it is proper that Americans focus their concern on withdrawing U.S. troops from Vietnam, where soldiers are dying and prisoners await release from Communist POW camps.

People must be informed about a subject before they can focus their attention on it. Well-meaning, but uninformed people are continually asking members of the families of prisoners such questions as: 'Now that the war is over, do you expect your son, (or father, or husband) home by Christmas?' or 'Does he say when he will be home?' or even 'Do you mean that they don't rotate them?'

The cruel truth is that the POW problem has been down-graded and de-emphasized by the top officials of our government. The people have been deluded into believing that the war is about over. The National Chairman of the Republican Party Sen. Robert Dole said that the war would be over for us when there are no more American casualties.

But will it be over for all those American boys held prisoner in Laos, South Vietnam, and North Vietnam, while we are still waging war over the skies of Southeast Asia, and while we keep a residual force in South Vietnam indefinitely?

In July, the other side made its announcement of the Seven-Point Plan for Peace. The first point stated that if we set a date for withdrawal of all U.S. forces from South Vietnam the prisoners could be released before the other points were settled. The total seven points would constitute a victory for them. They also said the seven points were negotiable.

Long ago our chief negotiator in Paris announced our demands for peace. These demands would represent a victory for us. We have not indicated that any point was negotiable.

So there are no 'negotiations' going on in Paris.

Neither our former representative at the Peace Talks, nor our present representative has ever mentioned the Seven-Point Plan except to ask them to 'clarify' their position. We have never asked the DRV (Democratic Republic of Vietnam) or the NLF (National Liberation Front) the following question: 'Will you release the prisoners and guarantee the safety of our withdrawing troops with no other considerations if we set a date for total troop withdrawal?'

Some say that we cannot trust the other side to release the prisoners if we set a date. I say that we have nothing to lose by trying— at least not now, while we still have sizable forces there.

And some of our American boys are beginning their eighth year in prison in North Vietnam. These are the men who are political hostages of the war. They are the ones who will be released when the war is over. They are the ones who are not mentioned by the politicians. They are the men who are forgotten by most Americans as they pursue their busy routines.

Now the families of the missing and prisoners are the only ones who desperately try somehow to focus attention on these forgotten men. I would like to persuade Americans to write the President and their congressmen as devotedly as they wrote to Hanoi.

My son has written one sentence in his six-line letter which must speak for all-'A day the sun rises, the sun sets.'

So, when the President of the United States and those who are candidates for the presidency say that the war is not an issue, when there is no news from the Paris Peace Talks, when very few letters are coming to us from the prisoners themselves, and when the news media refuse to discuss the prisoners, how do you propose we persuade the public to focus its attention on the prisoners-of war?" [4]

Along with the reply to Reston's piece, the newspaper printed the photo of Mark that was taken when peace groups were talking to him and a couple other prisoners. There was an explanation of who he was and who Min Lee was ending with the line, "The Times is happy to publish this as a 'guest column.'" [5]

Min Lee smiled as she read it over for a second time and thought about how many people read this newspaper and would see the photo of her son. It felt good. So many things these past few months had discouraged her or simply broken her heart. She was tired of the lies. She was very tired of the indifference of the military, the administration, and the general public. But Mark was still in North Vietnam. She could not, would not give up now. She didn't care who she offended or who she had to work with in order to get results. She would work with the Devil himself to get Mark out of that prisoner of war camp. She would do what she had to do, but my heavens, she was so exhausted.

CHAPTER 22

More of the Same and Then Some

The rest of the winter and early spring of 1972 seemed to plod along with Min Lee swamped with interviews—some positive and supportive of her position on the war and the POWs and some negative and accusatory. There were people who felt it wasn't her place to criticize the administration and urge for an end to the war. She followed the news on two televisions placed so that she could see both screens at the same time in her mobile home. As her head pivoted back and forth between the screens, she prayed for a break in the news for POW support. When she felt somewhat down she would look back at an editorial from the *St. Petersburg Times* printed in January. It read:

"Freedom For The POWs

'A good many families of prisoners think the President is using their sons as an excuse to stay over there,' said Mrs. Gerald Gartley, the Dunedin mother of a 27-year-old Navy lieutenant—one of 400 Americans known to be captured by the North Vietnamese during the Indochina War.

She may be right.

Because Mr. Nixon's highly touted plan to end the war, as revealed in a televised interview with Dan Rather of CBS, hinges on Hanoi's willingness to release the POWs as American troop strength dwindles to a 25,000 to 30,000 residual force. If the prisoners are not returned, even under the brunt of renewed air strikes over the North, America will not disengage from this misbegotten war.

And Mr. Nixon, in lieu of making good his 1968 campaign commitment to end the war, probably will turn to the American people and blame the continued conflict on North Vietnamese intransigence.

Why is this possible? Why might the North Vietnamese reject the swap of near-total withdrawal of U.S. troops for the freedom of the long-suffering POWs?

Because any deal that does not include the complete discontinuation of American support of the Thieu regime in South Vietnam is likely to fall on deaf ears in Hanoi. Since the close of World War II, the National Liberation Front and Viet Cong have fought against governments in Saigon supported by outsiders. As long as that support remains, there probably will be war in Indochina.

It is unfortunate that the United States was sucked into the Vietnam quagmire following the French defeat at Dienbinphu in 1954, and that, in the name of opposing communism, became allied with military despots Ngo Dinh Diem, Hguyen Cao Ky and president, Nguyen Cao Thieu.

The Rather interview fired speculation that the Administration was considering total withdrawal – POW return deal with Hanoi. That ray of hope was shadowed by Secretary of State Rogers' subsequent assertion that 'we are going to insist that our troops remain there, at least to some degree, until we have made every possible effort to get the prisoners of war back.'

Unfortunately, the effort consists of continued bombing of military targets in North Vietnam, which has served in the past to stiffen the enemy's resolve, CIA and Defense Department studies show. That this remains true is indicated by Hanoi's newly hardened line that an end to the Nixon policy of Vietnamization must accompany troop withdrawal if the POWs are to be returned.

The implication of all this, as Mrs. Gartley suggests, is the Administration still is not willing to return the political fate of South Vietnam to its people. White House concern for the prisoners of war is not equal to paying the price of their release and the release of American blood and dollars from a mistaken adventure." [1]

This editorial stated eloquently the whole problem in very few words. Min Lee did not understand why everyone didn't realize this. This year of presidential elections would be crucial to what would happen to the POWs. The subcommittee members in the League working for an end to the war were supporting Democrat George McGovern for president as he vowed to stop the fighting and bring everyone home. Min Lee and some League members tried any activity that would promote the idea of bringing an end to the war, such as letters to the Nixon administration, local rallies, and visits to local representatives to the House of Representatives in D.C. For example, Min Lee and Mary Doak, along with a young woman named Mrs. Hubbard, whose brother Cmdr. Randolph Ford was imprisoned with Mary and Min Lee's sons, presented POW bracelets to Republican Representative C. W. Bill Young, known as a moderate, and talked to him about reconsidering his support of Nixon's Vietnamization plan. The young sister of the POW was naively surprised that Young was so nice and yet had voted in favor of Nixon's Vietnam policy. [2] The threesome of Gartley, Doak, and Hubbard worked well together. They talked at a Lions' Club at the Fort Harrison Hotel in Clearwater, telling their audience that "Vietnamization abandons the prisoners." [3]

Min Lee was worried about Mark, but Jim was not doing well either. As Gerry had taken off for Maine for the opening of fishing season, in late April Min Lee drove Jim two and a half hours on her own to the Gainesville Shands Hospital after he experienced a particularly bad episode of mood swings. The doctors there put him on Thorazine, an anti-psychotic medication with many side effects. There were days when Jim was extremely anxious, and other days when he was like a zombie. Min Lee wondered if the stress she was feeling at this point about political things was negatively affecting Jim, but what could she do about it? She tried to have as much patience as possible around him and save her serious concerns about Mark for friends.

Fortunately, one of those good friends offered to look after Jim while Min Lee went to D.C. to attend a League meeting the weekend of May 6th and 7th. Min Lee wanted to participate in the group letter to Nixon that would be written at the convention. She wrote the following document to be distributed among the members:

"…AND MOST HAVE BEEN WRONG ALL ALONG

Two years ago, on April 20, 1970, President Nixon stated, 'We finally have in sight the just peace we are seeking.' Ten days later he ordered the invasion of Cambodia and, shortly thereafter, the invasion of Laos. Today he is conducting the most massive air and sea bombardment of the entire war.

The chasm between past prediction and present performance is deeply disturbing to any citizen wishing to believe what his government tells him. If the stream of erroneous predictions were based upon the highest level of intelligence then available, our intelligence apparatus is in serious disarray.

To emphasize the hazard of wishful predictions it is only necessary to compare what HAS happened with the following predictions as to what WOULD happen:

'There is no question that the Communist menace in French Indochina has been stopped.' Gen. J. Lawton Collins, Chief of Staff, U.S. Army, Oct. 27, 1951

'I would never send troops there.' Gen. Dwight D. Eisenhower, June 8, 1952

'I fully expect victory…after six more months of hard fighting.' Gen. Henri-Eugene Navarre, Commander in Chief, French Forces, Jan. 1, 1954

'The French are going to win. It is a fight that is going to be finished with our help.' Admiral Arthur Radford, Chairman, Joint Chiefs of Staff, March 22, 1954

'There is no reason why the French forces should not remain in Indochina and win. They have greater manpower, and a tremendous advantage over their adversaries, particularly air power.' Vice-President Richard M. Nixon, April 16, 1954

'I can conceive of no greater tragedy than for the United States to become involved in an all-out war in Indochina.' Pres. Dwight D. Eisenhower, Feb. 10, 1954

'With a little more training, the Vietnamese army will be the equal of any other army in its ability to combat the enemy and will be able to defend itself against the Vietminh if attacked.' Secretary of the Army Wilbur M. Brucker, Dec. 17, 1955

'The South Vietnamese should achieve victory in three years.' Admiral Harry D. Felt, U.S. Commander-in-Chief of Pacific Forces, Jan. 12, 1963

'Secretary McNamara and Gen. Taylor reported their judgment that the major part of the U.S. military task can be completed by the end of 1965.' White House statement, Oct. 2, 1963

'We have completed the job of training South Vietnam's armed forces…I feel we could wrap this thing up by the end of the next dry season.' Maj. Gen. Charles J. Timmes, Commander, U.S. Military Assistance Advisory Group, Oct. 31, 1963

'We are not about to send American boys nine or ten thousand miles from home to do what Asian boys ought to be doing for themselves.' Pres. Lyndon B. Johnson, Oct. 21, 1964

'We have reached an important point when the end begins to come into view – the enemy's hopes are bankrupt.' Gen. William C. Westmoreland, Commander of U.S. Forces, South Vietnam, Nov. 21, 1967

'But my friends, if in November this war is not over after all of this
power has been at their disposal, then I say that the American people will
be justified to elect new leadership and I pledge to you the new leadership
will end the war and win the peace in the Pacific and that is what America
wants.' Richard M. Nixon in his Hampton, N. H. speech, March 5, 1968

A diligent search has revealed only one statement which has proved
to be true. It is: 'I believe that one of the reasons for the deep division
about Vietnam is that many Americans have lost confidence in what the
government has told them about our policy.' President Richard M. Nixon,
Nov. 3, 1969" [4]

Maryann Fuller and Louise Mulligan, both fellow League members with
loved ones in Vietnam prisoner of war camps, helped Min Lee pass this out at
the conference. Others assisted in mailing it to all families of POWs. Louise
chaired a caucus meeting to go over it. Min Lee would later tell Gerry, "It
exploded!" [5] The next day members wrote a letter to President Nixon asking
for a meeting. Seventy members signed the letter, and thirty members went
to the White House to deliver it.

Min Lee returned home to Dunedin to find Jim asleep in his bedroom.
Her friend left a note reporting that he had been there most of the weekend
and had barely eaten anything while she was in D.C. Min Lee resisted the
urge to go in and scold him about how he could be where his brother Mark
was. How would he like that? But she simply sat down on the couch and
realized how tired she was, too tired to deal with anyone for a while. She
needed to fix herself a cocktail and sit in her rocking chair on the patio. She
needed to open a new carton of cigarettes, so she could smoke one with
her cocktail. She sat there too exhausted to get up and get her drink and
cigarettes. She would in a couple minutes. As Gerry had said now several
times—something has to happen soon for the POWs. Something. She was
tired of the rallies, interviews, and meetings. Tired of it all.

Min Lee woke up a couple hours later still on the couch. She listened for
Jim. No sound from his bedroom. One son imprisoned in North Vietnam;
one son imprisoned in his own head. It was too much.

CHAPTER 23

Moving On

A good cocktail, a good smoke, and a good night's sleep in her own bed helped Min Lee feel stronger the next morning. She felt even better when Jim came out of his bedroom as she made coffee and was delighted to see her. At breakfast she went over her upcoming schedule with her son even though she knew he wouldn't remember it. He kept smiling. When she informed him that she was going to fly back up to D.C. in a couple weeks and she needed to have him try to do better at eating while she was gone, he promised her he would.

First, Min Lee would have to sneak off to Orlando for a Florida meeting of League members. President Nixon had surprised Americans late in February by visiting the People's Republic of China with First Lady Pat. There he met with Mao Zedong about normalizing relations between China and the United States. Some pundits wrote that his intent may have been to drive a wedge between China and the U.S.S.R. Nixon announced a trip to meet with General Secretary Leonid Brezhnev toward the end of May.

The families at the Florida League meeting felt it would be a good idea to send the president a telegram asking him to address the POW situation with the Russian leader. The telegram specifically stated that the families:

"…strongly urge the President of the United States to make the release of prisoners-of-war and the accounting of the missing-in-action in Southeast Asia the first priority during his trip to the Soviet Union in May.

Since the U.S.S.R provides 80 percent of the aid to North Vietnam, we would find it incomprehensible that new trade agreements are being made at this time between the United States and the Soviet Union. These would put the United States in the position of extending credits and trade to a country that supplies the enemy. In previous wars there have been laws to prevent such action. United States military men have been dying for years while their country does business as usual with the enemy's supply sources.

We further urge that the release of the prisoners-of-war and the accounting of the missing by the only (Repeat only) conditions for complete withdrawal of the United States troops. If the problem of Taiwan is one to be settled among the Chinese then the problem of Vietnam is one to be settled among the Vietnamese." [1]

The group of Floridian League members also went on to talk about supporting McGovern for president. Many members signed the telegram that was going to the president, but not as many agreed to support McGovern over Nixon in the fall.

The threesome of Gartley, Doak, and Hubbard also spoke at a Mother's Day Rally in May at Faith United Church of Christ in Clearwater. Before the rally, the organizing committee issued the following statement:

"We are sad and can understand why mothers whose sons are still in Southeast Asia as prisoners or in the field would be near despair as a result of the latest step-up in the air war.

Sitting back year after year trusting that Washington somehow knows best and will bring the killing to an end is no longer acceptable. All women in the country must make their voices heard, and they can do it by joining together and shouting to Washington, 'No more. Stop the war now!'" [2]

At the rally, Min Lee and Mary spoke on their usual points about ending the conflict and bringing everyone home. When Mrs. Hubbard's turn came to speak, she told the audience, "We are all prisoners of war." [3] She went on to explain that Americans were "prisoners of the conflict." [4]

A clipping from *The Spectator*, a Greenville newspaper, was waiting for Min Lee when she returned from Orlando. Jim had pulled it from the mail and left it on the kitchen counter for her. It was entitled "Will Mark Gartley Go Forgotten?" [5] The article discussed the purpose of the Moosehead Lake Women's Club's project to make aware to the public that a man from their area was still being held captive in North Vietnam and a permanent scholarship for a deserving student needing financial help in attending college would be started with the class of 1972 in his name.

A handsome picture and description of Mark's school career made the article fun to read, but the quotes from club president Ruth Lang touched Min Lee's heart. Lang said in the article, "Hopefully, our project will help him (Mark) by making him feel his years away were fruitful and not wasted when he returns home. We want to get the whole town involved personally to honor him and we feel our project will be one step to aid him in his life adjustment when he returns, as difficult as the adjustment will be. The Women's Club is concerned with the young people in this area, we are also concerned with the POWs in North Vietnam, it seems fitting that we should combine our concern. Everywhere we hear of the generation gap. To get youth interested in the same projects as oldsters and accomplish a common goal we feel is a step in the right direction." [6]

The article went on to explain how the scholarship would encourage local students to excel in school, and it also asked for contributions to the fund. Ruth, you should be out campaigning with us, thought Min Lee. She also felt so pleased about the idea of Mark being alive and home. Mark had written in the last letter they received from him in February, "Hope with me for tomorrow." [7] Ruth was planning and talking about Mark's return as if it was really going to happen. We'll make it happen one way or the other, Ruth. I promise. Keep collecting that scholarship money.

CHAPTER 24

One More Plea to the Congressional Committee

What could I possibly say to this committee that hasn't already been said? Min Lee sat and pondered that question at her kitchen table. She should have been doing final grades for her high school students, but she had to get at least a rough draft of this testimony for June 1st's congressional committee meeting done before she could focus on school. This committee was considering the Democratic proposal of setting October 1st of 1972 as the date of troop withdrawal from Vietnam, contingent on the release of the POWs, and an accounting of the MIAs, and a promise of safe passage out for the U.S. troops. Secretary of State William Rogers had reported that the administration was opposed to this date-setting idea. They were demanding a cease fire covering all parties to the conflict as this was the only way to stop all the killing in Indochina.

Min Lee understood that she would be accompanied by Shirley Culbertson of Virginia, whose brother Commander Kenneth L. Coskey had been imprisoned since 1968, and Sheila Cronin of Florida, whose brother Lieutenant Commander Michael Cronin had been a prisoner for five and a half years. Min Lee knew they all had to display strong voices in front of the congressmen. She worked most of the day and finally had a copy of what she considered an acceptable speech. She read it aloud.

"Mr. Chairman, and members of the Committee: I am the mother of Navy Lt. Markham L. Gartley who has been a prisoner in North Vietnam since August 17, 1968.

I thank you for allowing me this opportunity to appeal to you and your consciences to show the courage to vote for legislation which would require the withdrawal OF ALL American forces from Indo-China with no conditions other than the return of the prisoners and a guarantee for the safety of our withdrawing troops, and which would end our involvement in this hideous war.

And I realize it requires courage today for anyone, of either party, to openly disagree with the President's policy.

Unfortunately, today it also takes courage for a member of the Congress to insist on the Constitutional responsibility of the Congress to have a voice in deciding the future course of the country in the great issue of peace and war.

Since the first American went into combat in the undeclared war-since the first American was killed-since the first prisoner was captured, the Congress has given explicit approval by allocating the funds without which the war could not have been conducted.

Only in totalitarian governments should one be afraid to speak out, and so I urge you, for the sake of my son and the other prisoners, to have the courage to vote for legislation to take us out of this war.

Presidents have come and gone, Congressmen have come and gone, yet this war goes on. How many more years can sanity-or even life- go on for those prisoners?

From remembrances of quieter times in America, from the safety of middle-age, and from the comfort of our homes we listen to talk from the White House, from China, and from Russia of 'peace for future generations.' I wish the President would go to Vietnam and talk of peace for this generation.

As a high school teacher, I am very aware that during the memory span of a whole generation of young Americans they have not known their country at peace. Since they have been of age to understand they have heard the daily 'body counts' with their evening meals.

My son had been a prisoner in North Vietnam for 955 days and nights the last time I pleaded with the Congress to take a stand on our ultimate relations with South Vietnam and not to sacrifice his life and the lives of the other prisoners in order to preserve a corrupt dictatorship in South Vietnam. By taking no stand, they have allowed him and the hundreds of other brave Americans to sacrifice more days and nights in a Communist cell. The most hardened criminals in American prisons are allowed mail, and their families may visit them. All except those condemned to death or life imprisonment have the certainty of freedom on some future day. Do you believe our men have faith that their government is committed to them? Are they smiling when they hear the bombs- as one pilot (now perhaps a prisoner himself) said or are they living in constant danger from those bombs and wondering if all the misery of the years since the heavy bombing in 1967-68 is now to be re-lived?"

Min Lee stopped for a minute and considered whether or not her wording was strong enough to reach her audience. She couldn't decide. She continued to read it as if she had people listening to her.

"Many of the families of the prisoners are frantic with fear that their men have lived through the hell all these years only to be in mortal danger from our own bombs. I question the statement of the Dept. of Defense that they know the location of the prison camps where these men are held if this knowledge is based on the same sort of intelligence that resulted in the Son Tay fiasco.

We have been told to be brave, and as late as last month an Administration spokesman told the League of Families that we should only work for humanitarian treatment for the prisoners during the 'interim.' But the prisoners have been made a part of the settlement of the war by both sides, and the 'interim' has now been eight years for some. Their families are wondering how committed our government is to these men.

On May 1st, 1970, the Secretaries of State and Defense, the Chairman of the Joint Chiefs of Staff, Gen. Westmoreland, and the Vice-President pressed our hands so warmly and assured us that the prisoners were the Number 1 Priority. Letters to the families assured them that every effort would be made in the highest levels of government to secure their release. Always, members of the Congress have told us in response to letters that they 'share our concern.' Several have told me that 'nothing is too good for those boys.' And nothing is what they have gotten!

On March 16, 1971, Sec. Rogers, before the Senate Foreign Relations Committee, was asked, 'Are the prisoners the only reason we would be leaving troops there?'

The answer of the Sec. of State on that occasion was, 'Yes.'

The next question was, 'So, if the prisoners are released or the North Vietnamese agree to release them will we get out?'

He answered, 'Yes.'

Sec. of Defense Laird told the New York Times on June 13, 1971, '…the President and I have agreed. I expect us to maintain a U.S. presence in Vietnam until the prisoner-of-war issue is settled…We are willing to take every American out of Vietnam providing that question is settled.'

We hoped so desperately that the other side would offer to 'release' the prisoners in return for an American withdrawal date, rather than just say they would 'discuss' their release. And finally on July 1, 1971 their proposal substituted the word <u>release</u> for <u>discuss</u>.

Since that time, and almost immediately, it seems our government's position changed.

Now the Sec. of State began to say that 'After all, the prisoners represent less than one tenth of one percent of all those killed.'

The families of the prisoners and missing were frantic last year when the war was 'winding down' and when Sec. Rogers testified in a Senate Committee hearing that it was a tragic fact that the prisoners could stay there indefinitely if there were no negotiations. And shortly afterward Senator Dole said on nationwide television that the war could end without negotiations and that it would be over for us when there were no more American casualties.

We have been led to believe that our government has offered a withdrawal date asking in return only for a release of the prisoners and the safe withdrawal of our troops. This is <u>not</u> true. All our offers have included cease fire and additional provisions which have the effect of preserving the position of the Saigon regime.

And what a crushing disappointment to those who <u>seriously</u> believed that the prisoners and missing really matter-for those who believed that President Nixon's promise to raise the question of the prisoners and missing when he visited China and Russia meant that he would, at the very least, make a guarantee of compliance to the Geneva Convention a prior condition to any bargaining with China or Russia. The bargaining was done, the deals consummated. Yet the war intensifies and nothing has changed for the prisoners.

<u>Now</u> we know that no one but us <u>really</u> care about our men. We alone in this country live constantly, during every conscious moment, with this war. We read every scrap of news, watch every newscast, and weigh every word of the leaders of both sides-desperate for something to give us hope.

No wonder we have lost hope. Americans are all confused as a result of the erroneous predictions presumably based on the highest level of intelligence, and on false promises made by our leaders.

I quote just a few- From a White House Statement, Oct. 2, 1963, 'Sec. McNamara and Gen. Taylor reported their judgement that the major part of the U.S. military task can be completed by the end of 1965.'

And Gen. Westmoreland, Nov. 5, 1967, 'We have reached an important point when the end begins to come into view-the enemy's hopes are bankrupt.'

And Richard Nixon, March 5, 1968, '…if in November this war is not over after all of this power has been at their disposal then I say that the American people will be justified to elect new leadership and I pledge to you the new leadership will end the war and win the peace in the Pacific and that is what America wants.'

All last year we were told the war was 'winding down' and as late as

April 25 the President said that Vietnamization was a success, yet on May 8 he ordered massive increase of bombing of North Vietnam and greatly increased American involvement because the South Vietnamese could not, or would not, defend themselves.

Just recently the Vice-President said that he believed we were about out of the woods. Just where will we be when we come out of the woods? Will we start the Vietnamization process all over again and wait another eighteen years until the Saigon regime is able to defend itself?

We have been told that we must stay in Vietnam for how else can we justify the deaths of nearly 50,000 Americans-over 20,000 since Mr. Nixon promised to end the war. I searched my conscience for the answer, and I cannot believe that the deaths of more Americans or the killing of more Vietnamese would make a mother's loss of her son any less hard to bear. If there is anything that would justify the death of those men and the years of sacrifice of the prisoners, it is that their sacrifice will prevent young men in later generations from being sent to fight wars we cannot win, in places we should not be, and for causes the majority of Americans cannot support.

Gentlemen, you have not 'sold' this war to the American people. I do not believe you have sold it to yourselves. If some are in agreement with the present escalation it is because they have been told that it will end the war. What will you tell us when the war goes on? What will you tell the families of the prisoners five, ten, twenty years from now when our homes are still empty and our hearts still heavy?

The Congress now has an opportunity to reassert its historic role as representatives of the people. Please, Gentlemen, at this turning point in history, assert your Constitutional rights.

I beg you to set a termination date for our entire military involvement. You have the power to do it. You are our only hope and the only hope for those prisoners who have suffered so much for so long!

End the war – Bring all the troops home and the prisoners with them."[1]

Min Lee heard applause as she finished reading her testimony to herself. She turned around and saw Jim standing behind the kitchen counter.

"What do you think, Jim?"

"It's a lot, Mom, but you make it sound great."
"I leave for D.C. in three days. Remember?"
Jim nodded.

With her final grades done for school, Min Lee traveled to D.C. and gave her testimony with two other League members—Ms. Shirley Culbertson, whose brother had been a POW since September 1968 and Sheila Cronin, whose brother had been imprisoned for five and a half years. No feelings of nervousness hampered Min Lee at this point. She was a determined and adamant speaker with a voice of experience and wisdom. She felt pleased with her presentation. Once again, after her testimony, Min Lee tried to speak to as many congressmen as she could find. Perhaps the fact that it was an election year made many seem somewhat more receptive to the public's thoughts about the war and the necessity to end it.

Min Lee returned to Dunedin tired and ready for a break up in the Maine woods. Of course, she would do campaigning for McGovern's election while up there, but the change to a quiet setting would be refreshing.

CHAPTER 25

Summer of '72 - A Season of Anxious Waiting

Greenville and Beaver Creek neighbors seemed different that summer to Min Lee. Some were still friendly and inquiring about the latest news of Mark, but others were rather cold and gave Min Lee critical looks. She had never felt completely at home in Maine even though she had been there for almost thirty years. She was teased about her southern accent. Gerry would make snide comments about her southern cooking as they stood with other people. "Min's baked beans wouldn't even make it with a bunch of workers in a logging camp in Maine," he joked. Neighbors' tone with her this summer was more than just the usual prejudice toward being southern, though. She decided to busy herself with McGovern campaign tasks.

The Greenville area people who loved Mark and wanted to show their appreciation of his sacrifice had been busy collecting funds for the Mark Gartley Scholarship. The first one would be awarded eventually to a deserving senior at Greenville High School. Min Lee spent a day in July sitting with Ruth Lang, president of the Moosehead Lake Women's Club, at a booth set up by the club at the annual Rockwood Sportsman Show. They both handed out pamphlets and other materials about the POW's plight. Contributions to the scholarship fund were also collected there. A couple young women made a point of stopping by the booth to show Min Lee their POW bracelets with Mark's name and August 17, 1968, the date his plane was shot down, engraved on it. Min Lee smiled whenever she thought of this for the rest of the season.

The idea of going to Hanoi to get a few released POWs suddenly appeared toward the latter part of the summer. Cora Weiss did not know who might be going or what POWs would be released, but she mentioned it to Min Lee. Cora and David Dellinger had spoken with North Vietnamese officials about this release that would act as a gesture of good will while they were trying to negotiate a peace in Paris with American officials. Min Lee was definitely intrigued by the whole idea.

In talking with Gerry about the possibility of the trip, Min Lee voiced concern over where Jim would stay if there was the opportunity for her to go. Of course, he could stay back in Beaver Creek when Min Lee went with the peace group, but what if Gerry needed to be involved in some way. It was possible that Cora might ask Gerry to participate in some last minute press conferences to provide a united front of both concerned parents. Gerry also decided he wouldn't mind seeing his wife one more time just before she took off for North Vietnam. Min Lee didn't mind that idea either. This all depended on whether or not she would be invited to go, she kept reminding herself. It was a big "if." She had to admit she was a bit nervous about going so far away and to a country the United States was in a military involvement with at that. She also was concerned about the needed passport and possible visa. Min Lee had never been abroad unless you counted Canada, Maine's next door neighbor to the north. She never needed a passport before as one could scoot into Canada with just a document of identification. They were friendly neighbors.

Gerry soon resolved the headache concerning Jim by finding some campers who would invite Jim to go back to Massachusetts with them at the end of their summer stay at Beaver Creek Campground. At the end of August with trepidation in the back of her mind, Min Lee packed just herself for the return to Dunedin and her teaching job. Gerry and Jim stood an extra-long time saying their goodbyes at the side of her car as she was ready to take off down the camp road. She missed Jim's company on the long ride down to Florida, but she arrived safely at the mobile home in record time with the aid of her "lead foot," as she heard Gerry saying that in her head.

Min Lee knew the opening of school would be a challenge for her. Her mind would be elsewhere. She worried about getting her classes planned and arranging for her leave if Cora did call. Even though her principal had been nothing but understanding and generous with her absences before, it could be a long trip this time. She fretted about what to pack. She might not be able to start her classes on September 5th before she had to scoot to New York for the trip preparation. Cora might want her up there as early as possible for interviews and other pre-trip things. She couldn't help but think of the danger of being behind enemy lines. She was concerned about so many things before she finally had to admit the plain truth to herself. The trip to Hanoi scared her. She bounced around in the living room of the mobile home trying to calm herself down by listening to the two different newscasts on her dueling television sets, but she wasn't absorbing much. Then the call came.

CHAPTER 26

Official Word

Cora's voice was full of enthusiasm as it came through the phone speaker. Min Lee had to hold the receiver a little from her ear. "We're going, Minnie Lee! The North Vietnamese are calling it a humanitarian peace act, and we are going! Can you come with us? Mark is one of the prisoners to be released. They told me at the last minute that we could invite a family member for each POW. What do you think?"

Min Lee tried to say how excited she was to hear this, but Cora continued on without giving her a chance. "The Vietnamese Mission in Paris called Wednesday telling me to come immediately to Paris with Dave for the final planning of the POW release. Remember me telling you that Dave Dellinger and I started negotiating for this with them back in July? I was with Peter and the kids on Martha's Vineyard when they called. I called Frances Fitzgerald, you know, the author of the book *Fire in the Lake* that you really liked, and she said she and her boyfriend would stay with Peter and the children while I was gone. Dave and I were on a plane the very next day! We had our meeting with the North Vietnamese on Friday, and they escorted us back to the airport the next day. While we were walking, one gentleman told me we could bring close relatives, like a mother, father, or wife with us to accompany each of the released pilots home. Dave and I haven't lost any time. We are putting together a delegation of people to help us. I'll tell you about each person soon. Right now, please understand we are leaving New York on September 13th. Come up as soon as you can." [1] They were talking on September 2nd. "Minnie Lee? Are you there? Can you go with us?"

Min Lee struggled to find her voice and then replied. "Of course, Cora! Of course, I will be there with bells on!"

"I have tons of calls to make! I'll call back with more details soon. Glad your Mark is one of the POWs." Clink went the phone. Min Lee stood holding the receiver for a minute or two. She had heard every word Cora emphatically said, but something inside her would not allow her to believe it. They were actually going?

She was still shaking when she put the phone down. She hadn't taken her hand off the top of the receiver when it startled her by ringing again. A familiar voice hollered at her. Holding the receiver even further from her ear than she had when she spoke with Cora, she relaxed a bit and said, "Hi, Gerry!"

"Good God, Min, the U.S. Navy just called me!" Now Min Lee grinned as he continued. "I won't believe it till I see him with my very own eyes, but they told me Mark is being released into Cora's custody. Of course, then they started with all their questions about Cora—'Did I know she was an alleged Communist? Did I know my wife was fraternizing with so-called Communists?'" Gerry paused and took a breath. "Know what I told them? If she's a Commie, then Commies are pretty nice, and we ought to have more of them around!" [2]

Min Lee listened as Gerry had a good belly laugh at his own joke. "I'm going, Gerry. Just finished talking with Cora. We're leaving out of New York on September 13th. At least I'll have time to prepare plans for my classes." Gerry was silent for a moment.

"Okay, Min. I figured as much if they'd have ya."

CHAPTER 27

Prep and the Trip

Min Lee didn't have a lot of time to sit around being nervous or scared as she hustled to get ready. She decided to simply take her lightest dresses and slack outfits, ones that would wash and wear easily. Those took hardly any time to pack. She prepared substitute teacher plans for a full month just in case it became that long a period of time. Her principal was his usual understanding self about her leave. But what occupied a lot of her time was the nonstop ringing of the phone at her mobile home. People with well wishes. People with advice. People with criticism of what she was planning to do. The persistent FBI and military officials. And then there was the press. Reporters from the local newspapers, radio and television stations competing with some more national press called at all hours of the day and night. They had no mercy. Min Lee didn't want to turn the damned phone off because she was afraid to miss a call from Gerry about something important, especially concerning Jim, for example.

There was also the concern about the bombing campaign that Nixon was waging in North Vietnam. Min Lee decided to call in an appeal to President

Nixon's military aide Brigadier General Brent Scrowcroft about stopping it temporarily while they were there. Scrowcroft told her the request would be passed along to Nixon. Min Lee heard the administration had done that for other special trips. She told the press in a phone interview, "A bombing halt would serve both as a gesture of good will and a safety measure for the three men. It would be ironic if after being held prisoner this long they were endangered by our own bombs." [1]

With her substitute teacher plans prepared for her absence, her bags packed, and word from Gerry that he had agreed to meet her, Cora, and David in New York for a press conference, Min Lee left Florida. Gerry would come down to New York and stay with her in a hotel for an interview on Thursday, September 5th. She unfortunately would have to race back down to Florida to pick up her passport and visa over the weekend. Both were promised to arrive by then. Yet another thing to fret about. But it was going to happen. Mark could be home soon.

The television interview went well, I guess, thought Min Lee. She had felt like she was in a dream. It just didn't seem real that they were actually doing this. At a last minute press interview the night before the trip, once again Min Lee was asked questions about the trip and her participation in it despite the objections of the State Department. Her answer was, "It is my opinion against theirs. I'm going ahead on my own instincts on what I feel in my heart is right." [2]

The travel delegation was all gathered. Min Lee felt immediately at ease with Olga Charles, wife of one of the POWs being released. She was a young woman about Mark's age. Min Lee knew of Charles' mother who had worked for peace groups, too, but couldn't come on the trip. Reverend William Sloane Coffin, who summered on an island off the Maine coast, was there and charming. A renowned international lawyer Richard Falk was joining them. An Associated Press writer Peter Arnett was on board. Before they all boarded the plane, they paused to thank a group of Families of POWs. They had gathered at the plane to give a sendoff of well wishes to the traveling delegation. Min Lee was thrilled to see so many of them there voicing not only approval of their actions, but encouragement. Then they were boarded and off. The first leg of the trip was from New York to Copenhagen in six hours. An eleven hour trip to Bangkok, Thailand followed that second stop where they stayed overnight. The next plane brought them to Vientiane, Laos and another overnight stay, before the short trip to Hanoi.

Min Lee took the opportunity at the stay in Bangkok to write and mail an aerogram to Gerry. In it she said:

"Dearest Gerry, I don't know what day it is. It is about 10a.m. Friday here. I believe it is about 10 Thursday night at home. It's <u>finally</u> seeming real. When we stepped off to ground in Bangkok I began to believe it.

Big press conference at Kennedy Wed. 7:30-8:30. Very moving. Other POW families from area came and were wonderful! Boarded a 'flying hotel,' Boeing 747, at 9:40. Our party is nine. Cora, David, Bill Coffin (Chaplain of Yale), Dr. Falk - law prof. at Princeton, Peter Arnett – a long time Asian AP reporter. A priest and a Catholic woman worker who are going to Hanoi to talk to Catholics there.

We have flown Scandinavian Airlines so far. 6 hours to Copenhagen going over Augusta and Presque Isle. Then met by European press – <u>crowds</u> of them. Stayed about 3 hrs in airport – a beautiful place. Then on airplane for 11 hours nonstop to Bangkok, Thailand, over Berlin, Hungary, Romania, (Istanbul) Turkey, and Calcutta, India. We have been given very V.I.P. treatment. This is a luxury hotel. Got here through 1 hr. traffic jam because of morning rush hour. Only stay until 12 noon for airport to go to Vientiane, Laos. There overnight and on to <u>Hanoi!!</u> and Mark.

I have been thinking of you all the time. I know what you are up against. I had it the past two years. I am praying so hard for you and Jim. Please keep up courage and take care of yourself. Surely better days and relaxing times are ahead.

All my love –
Min"

On a piece left empty on the left side of the small aerogramme, Min Lee added to Jim:

"A whole CBS and ABC crew travelling on same planes. The CBS rides 1st

class while we are tourist. Cameras and interviews very often going on. Hope you and Dad behave. I'll see you before too long." [3]

On the last flight from Laos to North Vietnam, Min Lee and Olga, the young wife of pilot Norris Charles who was to be released, sat together and held hands. Min Lee was in a modest, blue pants suit; Olga was dressed in a colorful, flowered top and slacks. They didn't say much. At one point Olga started crying, and Min Lee nuzzled her shoulder as a mother would. When they were approaching their landing place, Min Lee looked out the window over Olga and said, "Beautiful place. Unreal that they've been bombing it." She then smiled. "That's where Mark has been for four years." [4] They were finally there.

CHAPTER 28

Hanoi!

The travelers were greeted warmly by some of the organizations of North Vietnamese women involved in the prisoner release and other officials as they finally landed. Min Lee started to relax and look around when suddenly an air-raid alert went off sending everyone into a panic as the North Vietnamese hosts ushered the Americans into a cave serving as a bomb shelter. This time it was young Olga who comforted her older travel mate as Min Lee sat with her face in her hands while the noise of the bombing sounded around them. It did finally stop, and they were on their way to their hotel. In the car on the way to their lodgings, Min Lee was startled and concerned by the children, some very small, who ran close to their vehicles and tried to peek in the windows. Again, what was happening seemed like a surreal movie to her. She was somewhat rattled about losing her grasp on reality when it occurred to her she might be experiencing jetlag. This had never happened to her. The thought calmed her enough to smile at Olga and appear as if she were simply overwhelmed with the sights.

Once at the hotel, Min Lee and Olga were pleased to find out there was a beauty shop on the first floor where they could get their hair done the next morning before the official meeting of the prisoners and all the press that would accompany them at the event. They had their nails done while exchanging beauty tips with the North Vietnamese in the shop. The shop itself reminded Min Lee of beauty parlors of the 1940s back in the United States, and she sat happily with rollers in her hair when yet another air-raid alert began. This trip to the bomb shelter would be done with rollers on Min Lee's head and with Olga's hair only partially dry. Min Lee thought it was a very different environment in which to live.

After things got back to normal and with beauty prep done, Min Lee, Olga, and Cora, along with all the press and North Vietnamese officials, were escorted to an area where they assumed they would have the meeting with their POWs. Military escorts brought in the three Americans. There was Mark. Time froze momentarily for Min Lee. Then she smiled

"Better looking than I remembered him after five years apart," she said. [1] Mark blinked as if he was surprised, and then his mother wrapped her arms around him. He would later tell the press, "It was almost unreal. Not quite as traumatic as I expected." [2] Olga had already scooted around Min Lee and embraced her husband. She refused to tell the press what she had whispered in his ear as they hugged. The third POW Major Edward Elias stood and watched without a relative to greet him. Cora Weiss, who had been asked by the Vietnamese officials to stand in as his greeter, approached him, smiled, and said, "Welcome back." [3]

The North Vietnamese officials proceeded to gather the POWs at microphones set up to hear a comment from each of them. Min Lee stood in the background and watched as first Mark spoke and then Charles and Elias as well. All gave brief statements of thanks to the North Vietnamese for their release. They learned that this was all being done at the occasion of the twenty-seventh anniversary of the independence of Vietnam. They were reminded that it was to show clemency. [4] Then a commotion broke out as the relatives scurried to their POWs to hug and talk again. All were eventually escorted to a waiting motorcade to travel back to the hotel where they would have a banquet.

In the days that followed, the POWs and the peace committee gave several interviews. Peter Arnett from the Associated Press had accompanied the group and John Hart from ABC news participated in them. [5] During one informal interview, the POWs, sitting with Olga and Min Lee, were asked by an American reporter to share a memorable moment. Lt. Charles talked about the time of his capture. He said a North Vietnamese guard in charge of him patted his leg as if to say "it will be okay" [6] as onlookers came by to look at him and throw things at him. Mark laughed and spoke of being found dressed in all his combat gear by North Vietnamese villagers. He was carrying a loaded weapon with extra ammunition on him and a nice watch on his left wrist. The people immediately started squabbling over the watch while seemingly ignoring all his weapons. Major Elias related a story about testing to see if the North Vietnamese guards where he was imprisoned had a sense of humor. He asked for something to read, but he wasn't happy with what they brought him and complained. The guard who had brought the reading material informed him, "This is no university." [7] Elias told everyone that gave him a good laugh.

At a more formal interview with the POWs, Min Lee and Olga, and the peace committee, each POW spoke again. Mark and Norris Charles, both Navy Lieutenants, thanked the North Vietnamese officials again for releasing them and spoke of bringing an end to the war to promote the release of the remaining POWs left behind. Air Force Major Edward Elias, a few years senior of both of them, only expressed thanks for his release.

The peace committee, the POWs, and their family members were asked to go on some tours of bombed out areas. These were well attended by North Vietnamese press filming what would be propaganda materials. They toured the bomb damage in Hanoi, including the harm done to the famous teaching hospital Bac Mai. They also saw a destroyed Catholic Cathedral. After a few days of this, Min Lee spoke up and announced, "You people are going too far. If this keeps up, these men will look like collaborators instead of heroes." [8] The tours ceased and a farewell banquet was held back at the hotel for everyone. A Hanoi official toasted the pilots with "Friendship is almost too much to ask for. All we ask now is that you not be our enemies. We don't want enemies anywhere." [9]

Min Lee was anxious to get back on a plane and get out of Hanoi. She wanted her son to be on American soil. The peace committee had tickets for everyone on a commercial flight. They all boarded, the plane started to lift off the ground, and Min Lee finally began to feel some sense of ease. Now it seemed as if they would actually make it home safely. Finally!

CHAPTER 29

⚘

Going Home

The flight home felt entirely different to Min Lee. Besides the obvious reason of her extreme fatigue, both physically and emotionally, the difference in her mood had to do with Mark being on the plane with her. She smiled and got through the endless interviews of the traveling reporters on the plane flying with them while feeling less anxiety. The end of the journey was in sight. She planned to continue to work with everyone, including Cora and her groups, to end the war and bring home the remaining POWs, with all the benefits they deserved for their time spent imprisoned, but her biggest reason for becoming an activist was sitting on the plane with her and smiling and looking pretty good after four years of being in the custody of the enemy. It was also fun to see Olga happily smiling and keeping as close as possible to her dearest Norris. For the first time in several years, Min Lee had a feeling of contentment with the world.

The first stop they took was in Beijing where they stayed in a hotel that was closed except for them. The hotel personnel did open their small gift shop, and many of the men bought cashmere sweaters for gifts. The travelers were kept well fed but had no access to telephone lines out. A few games of ping pong were played to bide the time away while waiting for their next flight. Then in the morning, they were off to the Novosibirski Folmachevo Airport in Ob, Siberia where they changed to an international airline to go to Moscow. On their way out of Ob, everyone was taken by the views of the beautiful Ergaki Mountain Range. Min Lee smiled and enjoyed watching Mark's delight over the sites. She couldn't get enough of his handsome face.

At the Moscow airport much had been closed down. There were some arguments with CIA people there until a Scandinavian SAS, or special air service person, took the group to his home. They were served a huge meal and invited to make phone calls home to relatives. Mark and Min Lee laughed as they listened to Gerry's reaction to receiving the call from them. He had not been allowing himself to believe everything was going to work out until he had verification, he claimed. They told him to get himself down to New York. Hearing Gerry's voice on the phone in reaction to the fact that they were all right and on their way home was another big piece of the puzzle that was coming together for them as a family. Their host's driver with his van drove them to Red Square near midnight after that. It was lit up, and William Coffin played tour guide as they walked around.

The U.S. military appeared at the Moscow Airport the next morning and tried to talk the POWs into going back in military escort. There was a long discussion, and it was determined by the three that they should follow the lead of the peace group and go back with them, so the North Vietnamese would see their cooperation with their plan and be encouraged to offer more POW releases. Mark was for that plan as he did not want to do anything that would jeopardize the remaining prisoners in any way. Min Lee was proud of him. They were off the next morning in a plane that would take them to Denmark.

They landed in Copenhagen. They all rested there and got as ready as they could for the final flight to New York City. American diplomats once again talked to the three military men about taking a military flight home instead of traveling with the peace committee and press. Mark declined saying, "I specifically hope to go home by scheduled commercial aircraft so as not to jeopardize the release of any further men." [1]

Norris Charles also spoke up and said, "If you, the American people, want to bring [the remaining POWs] home you can do it. If you really want to end the war you can do it. I call on you to help me in bringing these men home." [2] They then boarded the SAS jet for the flight to New York. About two hours before they were scheduled to land, a Major Ronald Walker approached them and announced that he was the senior military representative on the flight. He asked Mark, Norris, and Edward to join him in first class to talk. The three men were offered military uniforms to change into for their landing. It was their choice, and they chose to put them on. They were informed they would be taken by military escort upon arrival to a nearby hospital where they would receive medical evaluations and debriefing.

The plane landed, and its door remained closed for twenty-five minutes while a heated argument occurred between Mark, his mother, and the delegation of military officials led by Dr. Roger E. Shields, Chief Pentagon Specialist for prisoner affairs. Dr. Shields informed Mark he would not get the two day visit with his family before rejoining the service that he had requested of officials in Moscow. Min Lee said, "We just want him to ourselves free of the Government, free of the Navy, free of the press, free of the North Vietnamese, and now we're not going to get it." [3] Min Lee found it too much to bear. She broke down sobbing. Mark leaned over her and tried to comfort her with his hand on her shoulder. A photographer snapped what would become an iconic picture that would break people's hearts once published.

Min Lee then said, "I haven't cried since the day you called me and said my son was shot down." [4]

Mark added, "My mother hasn't cried in years. You may have pushed this a little too far." [5]

The plane's door opened. The tarmac was covered with military police. A few close relatives were allowed in the area immediately surrounding the stairway down off the plane. The press was included. Major Edward Elias was first down the stairway and was greeted by his wife. Lieutenant Norris Charles followed him with Olga. He was accosted by his parents, with his father jumping up and down for joy as he hugged Norris. Lieutenant Markham Gartley came down last with David Dellinger, his mother and

Cora Weiss following them. Mark heard, "Look down here, son. You know what this is? This is the good old United States. You haven't seen anything like it for four years." [6]

Mark looked around for his dad. During their phone call from Moscow, Gerry had told him and his mother that he was flying down from the Bangor Airport with his friend and journalist Ken Buckley. Gerry found Mark first and engulfed him with a big hug around his neck. They had a minute or two to talk before the military officials approached them to ask Mark to go with them. A disagreement ensued between Gerry and the officials, but Mark and Min Lee told Gerry the military was being adamant. All three men, Mark, Norris, and Edward were taken. Min Lee stood clinging to her agitated husband. She held his arm and tried to soothe him as they both watched a line of long, shiny black cars carry their Mark away. He was taken from them again, but at least he was home.

EPILOGUE

IN THE NEXT SHORT PERIOD OF TIME, things were busy for all the Gartleys and the other two POW families. Min Lee would return to Dunedin to her teaching job as soon as possible. Gerry went back up to Beaver Creek to close down the campground. After being checked out quickly at the hospital, Mark, Norris, and Edward were taken by the military on a quick visit of each major television network, and then sent to different military facilities for more examinations and debriefing. Edward went to a facility in his home state of Georgia, Norris to one out in his home of California, and Mark flew with his mother to Jacksonville, Florida to St. Albans Naval Hospital. Mark would be a guinea pig in the military's new Project Egress, a program the military had been working on to help returning POWs cope with handling reentering society after a period of imprisonment. Min Lee was thrilled that Mark would be close by to her, so she could visit easily. Mark was glad to be near his mother, but he was startled to find the windows in his room at St. Alban's facility had bars on them. Mark asked them about the bars. His room was on the tenth floor. They told him it was to prevent returning POWs from jumping out.

The people in Washington, D.C. had been busy before the peace group even landed in New York City. A bill was passed on September 25th that made it illegal for relatives of POWs to travel to North Vietnam. There was also talk of possible court martial for the three men for accepting their early release through the peace group, but Secretary of Defense Melvin Laird decided against it. Six other POWs had been previously released. Gerry Gartley had been criticizing Laird and the military in general for their treatment of the returning men he called heroes, but he calmed down when Laird's decision came out. His son would be flying into Bangor soon

for a homecoming that would honor him properly. The press was agog
with articles, both positive and negative, about the release and the men's
homecoming. Some, like the national magazine *NEWSWEEK*, tried to
discuss both sides of the issue and please everyone. Even the League of
Families of POWs and MIAs was splintered over the issue. Of course, it had
been fractured into two groups, one on either side of the war issue, for a
while now.

On October 12th, Min Lee and Mark flew to Bangor, Maine and drove
up to Greenville for a homecoming the next day with 2,000+ town's folk in
the gymnasium of the Greenville High School. The downtown was decorated
with banners and flags as was the gymnasium. A young reporter by the
name of Bill Green was representing the channel 2 news out of Bangor to
report about the big event. It was one of his first assignments, and he still
remembers being impressed with Mark's composure during of the hubbub of
the ceremony. If there had been controversy in the town about Mark's release,
High School Principal Frank Tarazewicz dismissed it with a comment about
it not being whether or not to welcome Mark home but how. John Hanson,
the shop teacher at the school, had organized a fundraiser to buy Mark a
new car that was driven across the gym floor as the crowd cheered. Hanson
remarked that no one could give Mark his four years of imprisonment back,
so a new car was the least they could do. "Anchor's Away" was played as
Mark and his entourage walked to the podium to talk briefly to the large
group. Then Mark worked the crowd with a big smile and handshakes. NBC
news also traveled with him and his parents to Beaver Creek Campground
and filmed views of it and Moosehead Lake and Mount Katahdin. In the
background of the scenic views, Mark spoke of his love of the area and how
he had missed it so much that he even tried to draw it while in the POW
prison. The next week Mark would travel to Washington, D.C. as his parents
returned to their work. Mark would start a series of talks that would include
a speech to the League of Families.

Mark's talk to the League included pleasant exchanges on both sides,
including Mark's laughter about short skirts on women and long hair on men
in America to a plea to be cautious about what they said to the press as it had
been unreliable in its reporting and sometimes hurtful. He then went on to

give a brief summation of what happened to him as follows:

"I went to high school up in a little town in Maine, and went to college at Georgia Tech. I immediately joined the Navy, went into flight training. I didn't have a yen to fly as a kid, but the more I flew the better I liked it and it really became a passion with me. I was really a career officer, gung ho, and loved every minute of it. I wanted to get to Yankee Station as quick as I could, and was afraid the war would be over before I got there.

In August of 1968, on the second line period I was shot down north of Vinh in Nghe An Province. It was an experience, to say the least.

I was captured immediately, myself and my RIO Bill Mayhew, both in good shape, uninjured. We stayed in the general area for a couple weeks, and then we started north. And there was quite an amusing incident, they kept telling me a car was going to take me to Hanoi – a car. So, I took them at their word. I expected an old French Citroen, or some car. But that night when they took us in an old truck, tied us up, and away we went, myself, Bill Mayhew, and Paul Brown. It was the first time I met him. It was not exactly a good ride.

We arrived in Hanoi and we were separated immediately, underwent initial interrogation in Hanoi, and we were put back together again very quickly, within six or seven days for myself and Paul Brown, and Bill Mayhew joined us very soon thereafter, about three or four more days. We stayed in this group of three until 1969, before Christmastime, and then we picked up another roommate.

During this time we had moved from one camp to another once already. This is not an uncommon occurrence; people are shuffled around very frequently up there.

So, as I said, in 1969 we picked up a fourth roommate, a Major Roger Ingvalson, and we four stayed together from 1969 until October of 1970.

In between this time we were changed around again – twice, in fact. And we picked up three more roommates this time: Gene Wilber, Bob Schweitzer, and Ed Miller. We continued with the seven of us until October 1971, and we moved in with 20 people. We lost one man in a move before this; we now had 26 people.

As you can see, the group was getting larger. It was not uncommon. It happened to many people up there: the groups began to get larger and larger as the years of my captivity went by, and it made the whole thing much easier.

We continued in a group of 26 until the middle of April of 1972, when there was another shuffle, another move around the camps, and we became 18. And this of 18 I stayed with until the night they informed me that I was going home.

A few events surrounding just the actual release – activities at the time of release. Most of us – in fact, all of us of the older shootdowns -- there are two groups; the new shootdowns and the old shootdowns – so the old shootdowns always – we had ruled out the possibility really, of any release, especially in the "old guys" category. So they came by my cell and took me out and that's the last time I saw those men. I couldn't ever go back and see them. They had told me my family was coming over, and I would be going home.

It was a strangely unique and emotional experience. First, the idea of being able to go home and, second, having a family member come over to Hanoi and pick me up. It's indescribable.

The trip home was kind of a whirlwind-type tour. We went across China, to Russia, had kind of a mob scene in Copenhagen, poor control of the press, and a misunderstanding upon our arrival at Kennedy. But since, everything has been very smooth. I am very happy with the Navy treatment, and any of my requests that I've wanted – they've furnished me with cars, and just anything I desire.

Well, you know, it's been four years.

Before I get into any of the specifics of pictures and letters, and these types of areas which I know you are very concerned about, I'd like to give you a general broad brush on (a) the treatment, and (b) the conditions that existed first through the early part – now I mean "early early,) this is 1964 until the time I was shot down, and from the time I was shot down to the present.

I divide this into two areas. Treatment – I mean the actual treatment, physical, mental, this type of treatment by the North Vietnamese. And secondly, the conditions; i.e. the material; the sanitation, the conditions under which we lived during this period of time.

Starting out with the treatment, there have been many, many periods of treatment up there. They have run cyclic, depending on, mostly, some external conditions and sometimes internal conditions in the camp. In the early years the treatment was harsh. It was severe in many areas, and it was unnecessarily harsh in many respects. This does not necessarily apply across the board. Some men were not – they escaped this. Not because it was anything they specifically did, but it just happened to be the camp, the time area, and there were many, what you call – I'll try to get the right word here – it really depends upon the time frame you are speaking of, the camp you are speaking of, and, in fact, the American prisoners you are talking about. It's hard to make a generalized across-the-board statement when you are referring to these things, but I would like to dwell primarily on the last three years in particular. I am speaking now of the autumn of 1969 onward. Actually, about the start of 1970, and the treatment since then.

There was a policy shift. I cannot really or fully understand what the external conditions were, but I can give you a good idea of how it affected us internally.

The level of control moved upward into the hierarchy of the prison administration. The lower ranking people who were in charge of us had much less power. This benefitted us greatly.

There was a shift in many of the internal policies, for instance, the "no see" policy. At this point we were beginning to see other Americans. Up until this time it was impossible, and a punishable offense in many areas if you were actually looking at or seeing other people. This really shifted.

The food began to improve, increase both in quality and quantity. The group of men started very slowly to get larger. The isolation period was on its way out. The larger group concept was on its way in. They inaugurated the "good guy season," as we called it, from then on. And it has been flowing and increasing with cycles up and down. It's a cyclic curve, and the average is starting to go up since this curve.

Before that time the food, for instance, was adequate. It was enough to just maintain your weight. Now the food was of sufficient quality and quantity that you can gain weight, and some men whom I am very familiar with had to go on diets. I know it sounds hard to believe, but exercise doesn't get it all off. And particularly for their wives – some of the wives are getting a little bit heavy – and it really worries them, because now that they have acquired a 'schoolgirl figure,' they expect everybody back in the States to have one, too." [1]

Mark enjoyed getting laughs as he displayed how he got through those years of imprisonment—his sense of humor. He continued to speak of getting letters and packages. He talked of recreational opportunities, and some books. He also related the following incident about his mother:

"As you know, I'm a bachelor, and I was writing home trying to be very covert in my letters, and I said, 'Please send me some pictures of my beautiful old playmate.' I thought, well, sure, they'll get the hint from 'playmate,' it's 'Playboy Magazine.'

Well, what do I get? Well, first I get a picture of an old girlfriend – and she's been married and has three or four kids – and then I get a picture of my old college fraternity brothers – so finally I dropped the covertness and said, well, a pretty girl. One of the other things I tried was 'my beautiful young cousin.' Well, that was say over Mom's head. She didn't have any idea what that was." [2]

After his audience stopped laughing, Mark went on to speak of the POWs' knowledge of all the groups like the League were doing to help them, and he mentioned their concern about families at home. He was questioned about whether or not the POWs heard about the Son Tay Raid and said that they did and how they did. He promised to give information to as many families as possible. By chanting it, he had memorized a list of over 570 names of POWs imprisonment, he told his audience. He received a standing ovation when he finished his speech.

Mark and his mother Min Lee worked for POWs' benefits and care. Min Lee also continued to work on the campaign of McGovern that fall. In fact, Min Lee was an activist for the rest of her life for political and environmental issues, both nationally and in her home state of Maine. She became a beloved mentor to many fellow teachers and activists.

With some groups there remained a controversy surrounding the release of the three POWS. Richard A. Falk, an international lawyer, wrote an article for The American Journal of International Law published in July of 1973 by the Cambridge University Press that analyzed this matter of whether or not the release to the peace committee was appropriate. Mr. Falk writes in his article's summary:

"There is no way to resolve altogether this underlying set of doubts. We can, however, make an analysis of whether this release seemed generally reasonable in method and effect and therefore deserved implementation.

First of all, it was a consensual process. The North Vietnamese initiative was not repudiated, as such, by the U.S. Government or by the three men selected for release.

Secondly, there was some humanitarian benefit for the three families concerned and some degree of reassurance more generally felt, given their good health and positive reports of general camp conditions and morale.

Thirdly, there were no negative consequences to legitimate prisoner interests." [3]

Mark has shared how his plane was shot down in the following story:

"On August 17, 1968, my RIO (radar intercept officer) and I were leading a flight of two F-4s on a routine bombing mission on a PT repair facility on the coast of North Vietnam. We successfully completed our mission and were orbiting just off the coast waiting for our call back to the aircraft carrier for landing. We got a call from the radar ship called Red Crown saying that we had two bandits about twenty miles west of us at about twenty thousand feet. We turned west, dropped off our centerline tanks, went onto minimum afterburner and went after the Migs. We came in low at about ten thousand feet and got visual on two Migs above us on the right. The sidewinder missiles locked on and I squeezed the trigger. The missiles failed to fire. Now the Migs saw us and began evasive maneuvers. I glanced at my mirrors and saw a white smoke trail coming for me. It felt like sitting in a car with someone slamming the trunk lid down. I now had a left engine fire and no hydraulics to move the flight controls. We were inverted at about eight thousand feet when I called Mayday and pulled the ejection handle. The rocket seat worked and both of us were in our chutes heading for the rice paddies. We were captured immediately and were POWs.

For the first three years of captivity, I was beating myself up thinking that we had suckered into a fight with the two Migs up front and did not see the trailing Mig that shot us down. It was only after I got the word from a new prisoner that my wingman had panicked and shot us down that I finally stopped fretting about it. The news came as a relief knowing that we were not bagged by a Mig." [4]

Mark later heard from the pilot who was responsible for the friendly fire. They talked.

Mark went on to become a commercial pilot for Eastern Airlines, married a flight attendant by the name of Sherrel, and had four children. He brought his family home to Maine where he became Secretary of State under Governor James Longley. He ran for a congressional seat after that but lost, so he went into private business. First he worked for the large construction company CIANBRO as their vice president of operations administration, and later he was a manager of Cellular One. He often took his family to visit his parents in Beaver Creek, which had been incorporated into a township renamed Beaver Cove in 1979, especially in the summer. Gerry Gartley died in 1995. By then Mark was with his second wife Marcia. When Minnie Lee followed her husband in 1999, Mark made sure a program from her funeral was sent to her friend Cora Weiss. Jim Gartley passed away in 2013.

In the spring of 2021 while in his winter home of Fort Myers, Florida, Mark was going through huge, plastic storage boxes of his mother's collection of things about all her activism, particularly about her rescue of him. Marcia and he were preparing for a visit from the author of this book. The writer taught with and is still good friends with his second wife Marcia. They were all anxious to get out the remarkable story of Minnie Lee's quest to rescue her son. There had been a controversy between Marcia, Mark, and some old friends about whether or not his mom had actually been married before she met his father Gerry. In his search, Mark came across a shoebox-sized, carved wooden box. Inside he found several love letters written to his mom from a man who signed the letters simply C.C. or Cedar. Mark called this author and told her he thought he had found something important, but he waited to look again at the collections of documents in the box until the author was with them in Florida. The contents of the box revealed not only the love letters but a marriage certificate, a divorce decree after only a year of marriage, and a newspaper clipping that detailed the death of Minnie Lee's first husband. At last Mark knew why his mother didn't want him to become a top gun.

Today Mark is retired, in good health, and living in Raymond, Maine with Marcia. They snowbird to Florida in the winter. Over fifty years have passed and life goes on.

AFTERWORD

I COULD HAVE WORKED ON THIS BOOK for another five years after these first five years of research and writing. There are still loose ends. Minnie Lee's granddaughter, Marilyn Gartley, has requested information through the Freedom of Information Act, or FOA, about the FBI's involvement with keeping tabs on her grandmother during her years of activism. Minnie Lee talked of tapping noises on her phone calls and other things that led her to believe she was being surveilled. The agency has been slow to respond to the FOA request. At the time of the printing of the first edition of this book, Marilyn is still waiting to hear back from them.

Almost everyone who has graciously helped me with this project has more ideas they would like me to research and possibly include. The Vietnam War era was a complex period of time. One could study it forever and never really know enough to completely satisfy everyone in their audience. I felt the need to bring this project to a close, at least for now. My goal was to tell of the phenomenal work that Minnie Lee Gartley did between 1969 and 1972 to get her son and others out of prisoner of war camp and fight for their rights as POWs. I hope this book accomplishes that.

It seemed take the United States a long time to start honoring the people involved in this controversial military action in Vietnam. We now also need to recognize and honor the sacrifices and work done by the family members of these military servicemen and many other civilians working from home. The world needs to know about the Minnie Lee Gartleys who did so much for so little recognition. It was an honor to learn about you, Minnie Lee, and write this book.

ACKNOWLEDGEMENTS

I AM SO GRATEFUL TO MARK AND MARCIA GARTLEY, and their extended families, for giving me the honor of writing the story of Minnie Lee. I have learned a great deal about this remarkable woman and others like her who worked behind the scenes during the Vietnam War era. I would like to give heartfelt thanks Cora Weiss for her help, invaluable knowledge, and encouragement. My sincerest thanks also go to author Heath Lee for giving me the connection to Cora Weiss and for her help and reassurance about the nonfiction writing process. The patience of my writing groups, in Falmouth, Kennebunk, and Bethel, Maine, has sustained me when I was struggling. A shout out must go to four school friends, Jo-Ann, Rita, Paula, and Elaine, whom I have Zoomed with every Monday since the COVID pandemic. One is a computer sleuth, two others are experienced librarians, and one is just a wonderful cheerleader. They were able to either find anything for me or talk me off a ledge and steer me in a different direction when they couldn't.

I give love and thanks to my family, daughters Darcie and Kelsey, son-in-law Steve, dearest granddaughter Maya. As always, I owe so much to my biggest fan and supporter, my husband John.

ABOUT THE AUTHOR

CHERYL GRANT GILLESPIE has written or contributed to two other books since retiring from a forty-year career as a teacher. She was one of five authors who penned the anthology Compassionate Journey: Honoring Our Mothers' Stories, which was a finalist for the Foreword, Next Generation, and Book Fest Indie awards in women's and family relationship issues in 2019. Since then, Cheryl has published Gracie & Albert, a book about her parents' and family's struggle with her mother's mental illness. This book was shared with the Maine chapter of NAMI, or National Alliance for Mental Illness in 2020. A Maine native for life, Cheryl is a wife, mother, and grandmother. Find her online at https://cheryl-writes.com or https://www.facebook.com/memoirismything.

END NOTES

Chapter Three: Women Strike for Peace

1. "The History of Women Strike for Peace," Women Strike for Peace Website, https://womenstrikeforpeace.com/history/timeline.
2. Ibid.

Chapter Five: Protesters vs Activists

1. Jessica M. Frazier, *Women's Antiwar Diplomacy during the Vietnam War Era* (Chapel Hill: The University of North Carolina, 2017), 35.

Chapter Six: Best Christmas Gift Ever

1. Ken Buckley, "Iron Curtain Photo, Warm Hearts-Tell Family Missing Son is a POW," Bangor Daily News, December 5, 1969, MLGC.
2. Ibid.
3. Scrapbook notes, MLGC.
4. Ibid.

Chapter Seven: In the News

1. Cora Weiss Papers, SCPC.
2. Scrapbook Notes, MLGC.
3. Ken Buckley, "Hanoi Airs Maine Flier's Greeting: Aunt Knows Best," Bangor Daily News, January 1970, MLGC.
4. Ibid.
5. *Portland Press Herald*, 1970, MLGC.
6. Ibid.

Chapter Eight: The D.C. Convention

1. Georgia Tech Institute of Technology newsletter, MLGC.
2. Notes on League of Families of POWs and MIAs, MLGC.
3. Personal letter written by Minnie Lee Gartley, MLGC.
4. Personal letters received by Minnie Lee Gartley, MLGC.

Chapter Nine: Summer in Maine

1. Scrapbook notes, MLGC.

2. Ibid.

3. Ibid.

4. Ibid.

5. Ibid.

Chapter Ten: Trinkets to Tug at Heart Strings

1. "History of the POW/MIA Bracelets," National League of POW/MIA Families @https://pow-miafamilies.org.

2. Ibid.

Chapter Eleven: Son Tay

1. Heath Hardage Lee, *The League of Wives: The Untold Story of the Women Who Took on the U.S. Government to Bring Their Husbands Home* (New York: St. Martin's Press, 2019) 195.

Chapter Twelve: Christmas 1970

1. Pinellas Mobile Home Owners Association, Vol. 1, No. 2, December 21, 1970, MLGC

2. Speech written by Minnie Lee, MLGC

3. Pinellas Mobile Home Owners Association, Vol. 1, No. 2, December 21, 1970, MLGC

4. Undated list believed to have been published in Bangor Daily news, 1970, MLGC.

Chapter Thirteen: Becoming an Activist

1. Walter Lippmann, "Prisoners of War: Christmas Package," Newsweek, January 11, 1971: 20.

2. Ibid.

3. Ibid.

4. Small section of a Tampa Tribune article, MLGC

5. Heath Hardage Lee, *The League of Wives: The Untold Story of the Women Who Took on the U.S. Government to Bring Their Husbands Home* (New York: St. Martin's Press, 2019) 200.

6. Scrapbook of MLGC.

7. Ibid.

8. Ibid.

9. Scrapbook of MLGC.

10. Ibid.

11. Copy of testimony, MLGC.

12. Ibid.

13. *Miami Herald*, April 1, 1971. MLGC.

14. MLGC.

Chapter Fourteen: Meeting with the Enemy

1. Handwritten notes of Minnie Lee, MLGC.

2. Ibid.

3. Ibid.

4. Ibid.

Chapter Fifteen: Summer of Meetings and Press in Beaver Creek

1. "Another Mother for Peace," Another Mother for Peace website @ https://www.another mother.org.

2. *The Moosehead Gazette*, summer 1771, MLGC.

3. Ken Buckley, Bangor Daily News' articles, MLGC.

4. Ibid.

5. Ibid.

Chapter Sixteen: A Schism in the League of Families of POWs & MIAs

1. Notes from scrapbook, MLGC.

2. Ibid.

3. Copy of speech, MLGC.

4. Notes from scrapbook, MLGC.

5. Ibid.

6. Ibid.

7. Heath Hardage Lee, *The League of Wives: The Untold Story of the Women Who Took on the U.S. Government to Bring Their Husbands Home* (New York: St. Martin's Press, 2019) 212.

8. Ibid.

9. Notes from scrapbook, MLGC.

10. "Speaking Out," Time Magazine, October 11, 1971, 21, MLGC.

11. Ibid.

12. Heath Hardage Lee, *The League of Wives: The Untold Story of the Women Who Took on the U.S. Government to Bring Their Husbands Home* (New York: St. Martin's Press, 2019) 212.

13. Ibid.

14. Notes from scrapbook, MLGC.

15. Ibid.

16. Ibid.

Chapter Seventeen: New York and Dr. Spock

1. Martin Gansberg, "Thousands Join in War Protest," New York Times, November 11, 1971, MLGC.

2. Ibid.

3. Ibid.

4. Ibid.

5. Copy of speech, MLGC.

6. Copy of letter, MLGC.

7. Ibid.

8. Copy of Mark's speech, MLGC.

9. Copy of poem, MLGC.

10. Notes from scrapbook, MLGC.

Chapter Eighteen: Nixon's Lady from Florida

1. *POW Kin Losing Hope*," The Herald-News from Passaic, New Jersey, December 23, 1971, MLGC.

2. Copy of the broadcast, MLGC.

3. Ibid.

4. Ibid.

5. Ibid.

6. Ibid.

7. Ibid.

8. Ibid.

9. Copy of letter, MLGC.

10. Copy of letter, MLGC.

Chapter Nineteen: Media Splash!

1. Daniel Rapoport, "Nixon Loses Ground with POW Families," The Miami Herald, February 6, 1972.
2. Ibid.
3. Ibid.
4. Ibid.
5. Speech in scrapbook, MLGC.
6. U.S. News and World Report, February 7, 1972, MLGC.

Chapter Twenty: Keeping the Noise Going

1. *"Clergy, Kin of POWs Protest War at Capitol,"* The Evening Star, January 20, 1972, MLGC.
2. Press Release from the Fellowship of Reconciliation, New York City, January 20, 1972, MLGC.
3. Ibid.
4. Ibid.
5. Ibid.
6. Ibid.
7. Notes from scrapbook, MLGC.

Chapter Twenty-one: A POW's Day

1. James Reston, *"Vietnam Politics Continue,"* The New York Times, January 31, 1972, MLGC,
2. Ibid.
3. Ibid
4. Copy of editorial, MLGC.
5. No
6. Notes from scrapbook, MLGC.

Chapter Twenty-two: More of the Same and Then Some

1. *Freedom For the POWs,"* St. Petersburg Times, January 10, 1972, MLGC.
2. Virginia Ellis, *"Rep. Young is Assailed by Prisoner-of-War Kin,"* St. Petersburg Times, April 4, 1972, MLGC.

3. *"Relatives of POWs Hit Vietnamization,"* Tampa Tribune, April 8, 1972.
4. Copy of document, MLGC.
5. Notes from scrapbook, MLGC.

Chapter Twenty-three: Moving On
1. Copy of telegram, MLGC.
2. Peace Rally is scheduled on May 14," St. Petersburg Times, April 24, 1972, MLGC.
3. Allan Gengler, *"Mother's Day Rally Hits Vietnamese War,"* Tampa Tribune, May 15, 1972, MLGC.
4. Ibid.
5. *"Will Mark Gartley Go Forgotten,"* The Spectator, May 1972, MLGC.
6. Ibid.
7. Joan Crook, *"Mother of POW Finds No Comfort in War Decision,"* Clearwater Sun, May 9, 1972, MLGC.

Chapter Twenty-four: One More Plea to the Congressional Committee
1. Copy of testimony, MLGG.

Chapter Twenty-six: Official Word
1. Notes from Cora Weiss, CWC.
2. Notes from scrapbook, MLGC.

Chapter Twenty-seven: Prep and the Trip
1. *"Halt in bombing asked by prisoner's mother,"* Washington UPI, 1972, MLGC.
2. Henry G. Logeman, *"Mrs. Gartley Unconcerned At Objections,"* Bangor Daily News, September 14, 1972, MLGC.
3. Letter, MLGC.
4. CBS film footage, September 1972, MLGC.

Chapter Twenty-eight: Hanoi!
1. Notes from scrapbook, MLGC.
2. Ibid.

3. Ibid.

4. Notes from Cora Weiss Papers, SCPC.

5. Notes from scrapbook, MLGC.

6. Ibid.

7. Ibid.

8. Ibid.

9. Ibid.

Chapter Twenty-nine: Going Home

1. *"The Battle of the POWs,"* Newsweek, October 9, 1972, MLGC.

2. Ibid.

3. Seymour M. Hersh, *"3 Freed P.O.W.'s Return; Dispute Flares Over Leave."* New York Times, October 29, 1972.

4. Ibid.

5. Ibid.

6. Notes from Scrapbook, MLGC.

Epilogue

1. Transcript of speech, MLGC.

2. Ibid.

3. Richard A. Falk, *"International Law Aspects of Repatriation of Prisoners of War During Hostilities,"* An American Journal of International Law, Vol. 67, No.3, July 1973.

4. Words of Markham Gartley.

SELECTED BIBLIOGRAPHY

Archives and Special Collections

Note: The abbreviations used in the notes for archival sources, both public and private, are listed below.

SCPC   Swarthmore College Peace Collection, Swarthmore, PA, Papers of Cora Weiss and David Dellinger were reviewed.

MLGC   Minnie Lee Gartley Collection, private collection, ME

CWC   Cora Weiss Collection, private collection, NY

Author Interviews

Note: All interviews done between 2018 and 2022.

Buckley, Ken

Bunker, Steve

Cunningham, Roxanne

Farrand, Sally

Flahive, Jean

Green, Bill

Weiss, Cora

Selected Articles

Buckley, Ken, "Iron Curtain Photo, Warm Hearts-Tell Family Missing Son is a POW." *Bangor Daily News*, December 5, 1969.

Buckley, Ken, "Hanoi Airs Maine Flier's Greeting-Aunt Knows Best." *Bangor Daily News,* January 1970.

Falk, Richard A., "International Law Aspects of Repatriation of Prisoners of War during Hostilities." *The American Journal of International Law*, Vol. 67, No. 3 (July, 1973).

Gansberg, Martin, "Thousands Join in War Protest." *New York Times*, November 7, 1971.

Hersh, Seymour M., "3 Freed P.O.W.'s Return; Dispute Flares over Leave."

New York Times, October 29, 1972.

Lippmann, Walter, "Prisoners of War: Christmas Package." *Newsweek*, January 11, 1971.

"The Battle of the POWS." *Newsweek*, October 9, 1972.

Rapoport, Daniel, "Nixon Loses Ground with POW Families, *The Miami Herald*, February 6, 1972.

Websites

"Another Mother for Peace," Another Mother for Peace website@ https://www.anothermother.org.

Smithsonian Magazine @https://www.smithsonianmag.com/smart-news/notes-indicate-nixon-interferred-1968-peace-talks-180961627.

"The History of Women Strike for Peace," Women Strike for Peace Website @https://womenstrikeforpeace.com/history/timeline.

"The History of the POW/MIA Bracelets," National League of POW/MIA Families website @https://pow-miafamilies.org.

Videos and Television Programs

The Vietnam War, PBS, September 2017, Burns, Ken and Novick, Lynn.

CBS news clips, peace group's trip to Hanoi and back, September 1972, MLGC.

NBC News, reported by Frank Bourgholtzer, October 14, 1972. Mark Gartley's homecoming, Greenville, Maine, MLGC.

Books

Clinton, James W. The Loyal *Opposition: Americans in North Vietnam, 1965-1972*, Niwot: University of Colorado, 1995.

Fitzgerald, Frances. Fire in the Lake: *The Vietnamese and the Americans in Vietnam*, Boston: An Atlantic Press Book Monthly, 1972.

Frazier, Jessica M. *Women's Antiwar Diplomacy during the Vietnam War Era*,

Chapel Hill: The University of North Carolina Press, 2017.

Lee, Heath Hardage. *The League of Wives: The Untold Story of the Women Who Took on the U.S. Government to Bring Their Husbands Home*, New York: St. Martin's Press, 2019.

Kraslow, David and Loory, Stuart H. *the Secret Search for Peace* in Vietnam, New York: Vintage Books: A Division of Random House, 1968.

Swerdlow, Amy. *Women Strike for Peace*, Chicago: The University of Chicago Press, 1993.

Taylor, Ethel Barol. *We Made a Difference*, Philadelphia: Camino Books, Inc., 1998.

Vietnamese Studies. *Vietnamese Women*, Hanoi: Democratic Republic of Vietnam-Xunhasaba, 1966.

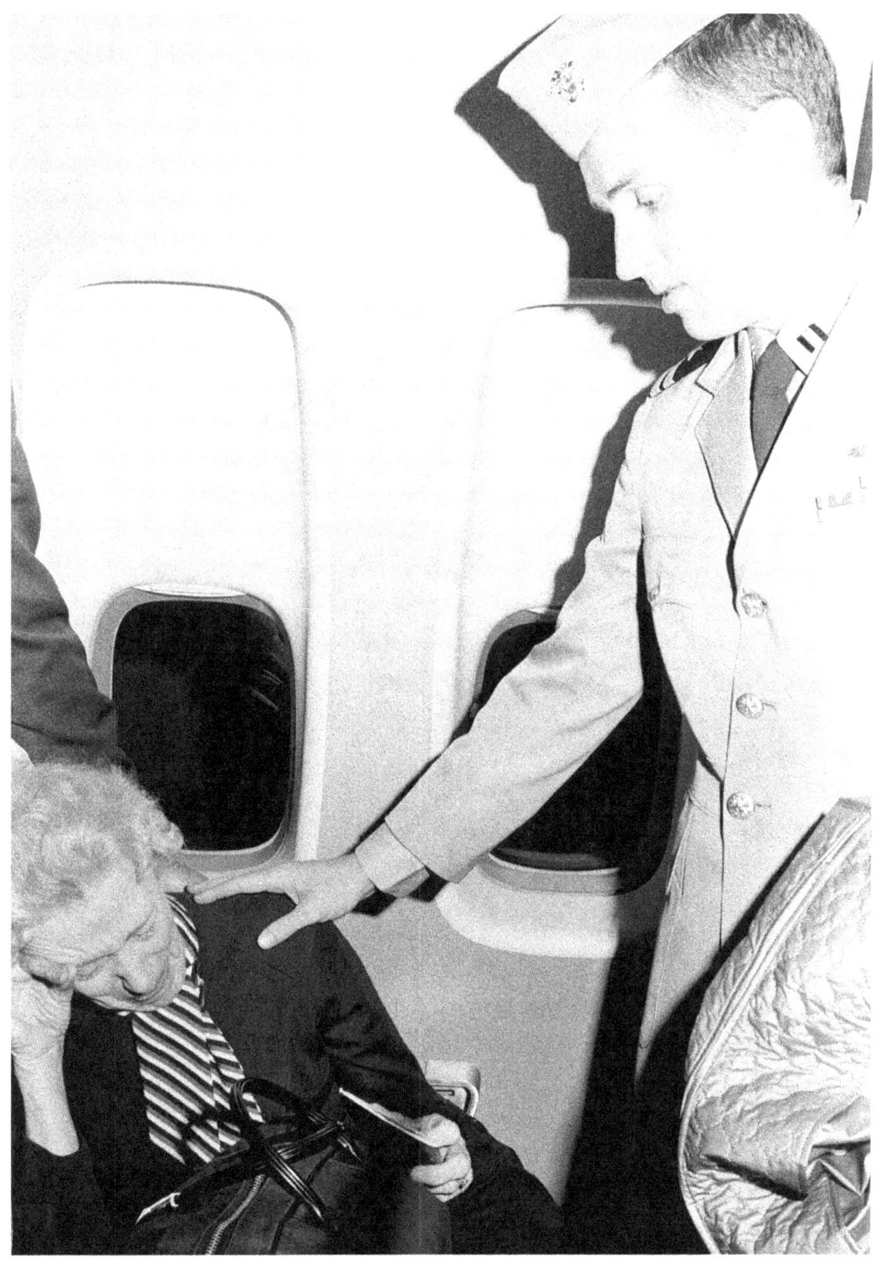

AP Photos

Mark comforting his mother on the plane

MLGC

Mark and navigator Bill Mayhew

MLGC

Minnie Lee as a young woman

MLGC

Minnie Lee and Mark, 1944

MLGC

Minnie Lee and Gerry in Memphis, 1942

Cora Weiss

Traveling group in Beijing, Peter Arnett, Minnie Lee Gartley, Cora Weiss, Olga Charles, Richard Falk, Lieutenant Norris Charles, David Dellinger, Lieutenant Mark Gartley, Major Edward Elias

MLGC

Postcard of the camp